PRECIOUS DAYS
&
PRACTICAL LOVE

CARING FOR
YOUR
AGING PARENT

JAMES TAYLOR

PRECIOUS DAYS
& PRACTICAL
LOVE
CARING
FOR YOUR
AGING PARENT

Northstone

EDITORS: Michael Schwartzentruber, Dianne Greenslade
COVER AND INTERIOR DESIGN: Margaret Kyle
CONSULTING ART DIRECTOR: Robert MacDonald
Cover Art: leaves from an award-winning quilt by Edith Quinn called *After the Harvest*,
Edmonton, AB, Canada. Used by permission.

Northstone Publishing acknowledges the financial support of the Government of Canada,
through the Book Publishing Industry Development Program, for its publishing activities.

Northstone Publishing is an imprint of Wood Lake Books Inc., an employee-owned company,
and is committed to caring for the environment and all creation. Northstone recycles, reuses, and
composts, and encourages readers to do the same. Resources are printed on recycled paper and
more environmentally friendly groundwood papers (newsprint), whenever possible.
The trees used are replaced through donations to the Scoutrees for Canada program.
A percentage of all profit is donated to charitable organizations.

CANADIAN CATALOGUING IN PUBLICATION DATA
Taylor, James, 1936-
Precious days & practical love
Includes bibliographical references and index.
ISBN 1-896836-34-8
1. Aging parents – Care. 2. Parent and adult child. 3. Caregivers –
Family relationships. I. Title. II. Precious days and practical love.
HQ1063.6.T39 1999   306.874   C99-910826-3

Published by Northstone Publishing
an imprint of Wood Lake Books, Inc., Kelowna, BC Canada

Printing 10 9 8 7 6 5 4 3 2 1
Printed in Canada by Transcontinental Printing

DEDICATION

To my father
William Stephens Taylor
February 23, 1905 – August 16, 1998

And the days dwindle down
To a precious few
September, November…
And these last precious days,
I'll spend with you,
These precious days
I'll spend
With you.

from *September Song* [©]
by Maxwell Anderson and Kurt Weill.

TABLE OF CONTENTS

The Final Relationship

On January 28, 1998, my life changed. Irrevocably.

My wife, Joan, and I came home from a winter holiday, to learn that my father was in the hospital. He had suffered two heart attacks.

In the weeks and months that followed, we learned what it means to take responsibility for an aging and dying parent. This experience comes to most of us only once in our lives. There is, therefore, no way to prepare for it. Nor is there much that makes the experience a training ground for other life experiences. It's often a "one shot" situation – if you miss the target this time around, you don't get any second chances.

It's also an intensely emotional experience. That's why I wrote this book. In doing my research, I talked with and interviewed, formally or informally, at least 30 people – my notebook became dog-eared and started losing pages before I finished. All of the people had bits of practical wisdom to offer. But what obsessed all of them (whether or not they wanted to talk much about it) was the emotional roller coaster that they found themselves on. "I don't mind talking about my mother," one woman commented, "as long as you don't mind me bursting into tears unpredictably."

The practical steps

There are quite a few books out there that can tell you what to do. There are literally hundreds of associations and agencies, and probably millions of lawyers and accountants, all of whom can offer practical advice and counsel. But I can summarize the basic message very simply.

While you still can, communicate with your parent

- Make sure your parent has a valid, up-to-date will. Know where it is.
- Find out where all bank accounts, insurance policies, and investments are.
- Get a Power of Attorney, for the time when the parent can no longer manage his or her own affairs.
- Learn what kind of care your parent wants, when there's no longer any expectation of recovery.
- Arrange for care – nursing or personal – as necessary.
- Discuss what kind of funeral arrangements your parent would like.
- Keep other family members and relatives informed.
- Transfer some accounts and assets into joint ownership.

What to do after death, if you're named as executor

- Notify relatives and friends.
- Arrange for the funeral or memorial service.
- Get a notarized copy of the parent's will and a number of notarized copies of an official death certificate.
- Notify all accounts and institutions, including government and pension agencies, of the death.
- Notify all potential beneficiaries, whether named in the will or not, of the will's provisions.
- List all of your dead parent's assets and liabilities.
- Using the appropriate forms and procedures for your state or province, apply for Letters Probate (or whatever other name your particular jurisdiction uses), which legally authorize you to act on behalf of your parent's estate.

- Submit a final income tax declaration for your parent, up to the date of death.
- Pay the government any taxes owing.
- Divide up the estate according to the instructions of the will.

And if you are neither a primary caregiver nor the executor

- Keep informed. Keep in touch.
- Don't meddle. Don't assume that you and you alone know what's best for your parent.
- Accept your share of responsibilities.
- Avoid family squabbles and sibling rivalries. The last thing a declining parent needs is to get entangled in a family feud, or to watch a family disintegrate into hostilities.
- Intervene only if it seems clear that the primary caregiver or executor is no longer acting on the parent's behalf, but is manipulating either the parent or the parent's estate for personal gain.
- Learn to recognize the symptoms of grieving in others and in yourself. Offer compassion and understanding.

An emotional time

That's the summary. Put in those terms, it all sounds very straightforward, very dispassionate. And that's totally misleading. If it were just a matter of dealing with legal and financial requirements, anyone of average intelligence could handle the tasks.

But this situation doesn't call for just "anyone." It calls for you, and no one else. You are this parent's child; this person is your father or mother. This is the woman who suckled you at her breast and held your hand as you went off to school. This is the man who took you fishing and walked the floor holding you in his arms in the middle of the night. You will never have another father or mother.

In other words, this is all about relationships. And relationships are all about emotions. Ideally, they're about love. But sometimes, even in the best of families, they involve rebellion and rejection, hurt and abuse, pain and loss of self-esteem. All of those factors will enter into this final relationship. How you work them out will determine whether these final months or years are among the best or the worst experiences of your life.

For these reasons, this book is unabashedly emotional. I could simply cite authorities. I could rely on other published sources. But doing that would attempt to make this book objective, unemotional, and impersonal.

What I found missing in the other books I read was the pain of watching someone you love fade away to nothing. Of being unable to change the inevitable. But of still having an inner compulsion to do what you can, to make those final weeks or months or years as easy and gentle as possible. Of having your roles reversed, so that you find the person you've depended on all your life now depending on you. And of continuing to love, when the person you love can no longer love you back.

Among the people I interviewed, the thing that they talked about, that they needed to talk about, was the emotion they felt. Not the tasks they performed.

I write a local newspaper column. Without fail, the columns that draw the most response – enough for people to come out of their homes when they see me going by walking the dog, enough for people to flag me down on the road – are the ones raw with emotion.

So that's what I decided to write. Even though writing this book has felt, at times, like reopening wounds that were just beginning to heal.

Sacrificing my father for a cause

I couldn't have written this book if my father were still alive – he would not want to have his weakness, his inability, revealed for all to see. Time and again, when he found himself unable to control his bowels, when he couldn't get up to welcome a visitor, when he couldn't keep track of his checks, he broke down in tears, whispering, "I'm sorry. I'm so sorry." He did not like being less than himself.

In a sense, I'm sacrificing him for a cause. I have written about him in terms that he would probably not welcome – and in that sense, he represents all of us. For all of us, there comes a decline in our capabilities as we approach the end of life. And we might as well face that fact. The description of us, as we wind down, is not likely to be flattering either. I could have created fictional cases, as some authors do. But somehow, those cases never quite ring true – readers have an uncanny ability to recognize phony examples. Or I could have selected stories about distant third parties whom no one knows personally. But that means no one actually cares about them, either.

I cared deeply about my father. I hope that feeling will show in these pages.

I hope, too, that in writing about my father as I have, I have not offended his friends and former colleagues. I hope they will still see, in the man I have depicted, the man they knew and admired. I trust they will still recognize, even in weakness, his wit, his dry humor, his wide-ranging interests.

And after death...

I am not worried about offending Dad himself. He harbored no illusions that after he died, he would still hang around this earth watching the rest of us from behind some kind of invisible veil. When this life was over, it was over. Period.

What lay beyond this life, he did not know. And he was content not to know.

In one of his books (*Seeing the Mystery,* Wood Lake/Novalis, 1989) he wrote about a painting of Jesus by Father Jerome Esser. The words strike me as a summary of his life and his faith.

I suddenly found a face before me. The background is dark, shadowed, opaque. But out of those shadows emerges a face, with white skin, chestnut-colored hair, parted in the middle, a beard…Somewhere, there's a dark blue cape or coat, but I have to force myself to look for that.

For I cannot take my eyes from the face. The mouth, so firm yet so gentle. It almost seems ready to open, to speak. And the eyes. Deep, brown, they look straight into mine, seeing the depths of my soul. I cannot tear myself away.

What makes those eyes so inescapable? I don't know. I have looked at hundreds of pictures of Christ's face, as artists have imagined it, both in the Eastern and Western churches. I have never seen eyes that haunt me like these. They will not let me go, yet they do not hold me against my will.

The background is so dark, so lacking in detail, I cannot tell whether the face is large or small, near or far. Nor do I care. For in following, I will know more. And yet the more I know of him, the more I see of him, the more his mystery will continue to elude my groping.

This is the man of mystery, looming out of the darkness of the unknown. He is compelling. He is appealing.

Peace, peace…I follow…

He did follow. And I believe he found peace.

Self-discovery

As you read these pages, I hope you'll cry. I hope you'll laugh. I hope you'll nod your head, and say, "Yes, me too." And in the process, I hope you'll learn – about your responsibilities, about yourself, and about your present relationship with your parent.

"And the days dwindle down," say the lyrics to *September Song*, "to a precious few." Although the song was written about a romance spanning the ages, the sentiment holds true for parent/child relationships too. There comes to all of us, at some time, a startling realization that the days *do* dwindle down, that the relationship must end, that the remaining days are numbered, even if we have no idea what that number may be.

I write this book in the hope that the final relationship – however long it may be – can turn out to be "precious days."

ONE

The Parental Cover-Up

As long as both parents are alive, the stronger one will cover for the weaker one. Not until you only have one parent left, will you learn what it really means to care for an aging parent. And then you'll have to learn as you go.

Biologically, all of us had two parents. In practice, you may have had one, or two, or more – given the numbers of multiple marriages, blended families, and single-parent families these days. But in your parents' generation, two-parent families were the norm.

Although you have two parents, the chances are that when those parents grow old, you will end up caring for only one of them. When the first parent's health declines, the other parent usually becomes the primary caregiver. Unless you happen to live right next door, you will probably never know just how much care that second parent provides for the declining one.

Perhaps the most common phrase I heard in all my interviews was, "We had no idea…" No idea how much he had helped her pick out her clothes. How often she had answered questions for him. Why he always went to the supermarket with her, to keep her from getting lost in the parking lot. Or why she always paid the bills…

As one woman said to me, "Mum looked after Dad for 56 of their 58 years of marriage!"

The real shock comes when the protective parent dies, and leaves the dependent one alive. That's when you try to tell him he's going to have to remember to zip up his fly – and discover he's no longer capable of learning new habits. That's when you remind her that she has to turn the stove off after cooking her dinner – and you have to remind her again the next day, and the next, and the next after that…

That's why caring for an aging parent is usually a "first time" experience. As a child, you don't get a dress rehearsal. Most often, your other parent will have insulated you, perhaps deliberately protected you, from being the primary caregiver.

I had no idea…

I should have had plenty of opportunity to know what it's like to look after a declining parent. But I still didn't know, until I was down to one last parent.

My father, you see, outlived two wives. My biological mother died when I was 36. At the time, both of my parents lived in Vancouver; I had a job and a home in Toronto. I knew she was sick – I had no idea how sick.

My father wrote about in it a sort of memoir that he prepared for his granddaughter, our daughter Sharon.

1971 ushered Mary and me into the most difficult, heartbreaking period of our lives together. When I came back [from a national church meeting in eastern Canada], Mary took me aside. She took my hand and held it against her upper abdomen, just below the ribs. "Feel here," she said.

I did feel there, and I was shocked. I felt a hard lump. "What's this?" I asked. "How long have you had it?"

She had learned about it, she said, early in the year. But she had said nothing because she was afraid, if I knew of it, I would refuse to go to the meetings…

She was right; I would not have gone. It was a wonderfully loving and self-abnegating act on Mary's part. But I wished she had not done it.

The lump turned out to be cancer, Hodgkin's disease. By the time she had it checked out, it had spread too far for treatment by surgery. Ten months of x-ray and chemotherapy followed. My mother lost her hair. She lost control of her bowels. She lost weight. By that summer she was, Dad noted later, "almost skeleton thin." Dad drove her back and forth to the hospital. As she grew weaker, he carried her up and down the stairs in their home, and eventually converted a room on the ground floor to be her bedroom. In spite of having a full-time job as principal of a theological college, he devoted enormous amounts of time to her.

But I, far away in Toronto, knew almost nothing of this. I got letters – but in them my mother kept any upsetting news from us, just as she had kept the growth of her tumor from my father.

She didn't actually go into hospital until her final week of life. In those days, I worked for *The United Church Observer*, the United Church of Canada's national magazine. The *Observer* sent me to Vancouver to report and write a couple of articles. By coincidence, I arrived the day my mother went into hospital. She died five days later, almost exactly one year after she had instructed Dad to feel the lump in her abdomen.

Dad and I had spent most of that final day at the hospital with her. But that evening Dad was being installed as the first principal of the new Vancouver School of Theology. We left the reception early. Neither of us, Dad wrote later, "could face drinking cups of tea while Mary lay dying without us. When we got back to the hospital, Mary had passed beyond knowing we were there. At midnight, the doctor sent us home… At two o'clock the next morning, he phoned to tell me Mary had died."

I woke at 7:00 a.m., as I felt a weight settle on the side of my bed. I opened my eyes to see Dad sitting there. And I knew what had happened. Typically, he hadn't wakened me when the news first came in. Rather than disturb me, he had read the gospels all the way through, seeking comfort not so much in any verbal message contained there as in the familiar cadence of the words, much as others might listen to Mozart.

He held me as if I were still a small child, and we sobbed on each other's shoulders.

One more time

Incredibly, he went through the same experience a second time. Four years after my mother died, my father married Christina Fraser. He was 71; she was 68. Given their ages, they were realistic; they knew their time together would be limited. They didn't know how limited, though.

Five years later, Chris developed kidney failure. This time, we knew enough to ask a bit more about the kind of care Dad was giving her, but even so, we remained blissfully ignorant of most of it. We knew that peritoneal flushing at home gradually turned into full-fledged dialysis – weekly to begin with, increasing to daily. Chris became almost helpless. When she fell out of bed, Dad had to lift her physically back in – despite recovering from his first heart attack. Chris never even knew that she had fallen out of bed. Finally, her liver gave up too, and there was nothing more that dialysis could do for her.

She and Dad agreed not to take any extraordinary measures to sustain her life. When the time came, she would go. But on the last day, he told us, he sat with his arm around her shoulders, holding her up, encouraging her to take one more sip of soup to keep her strength up.

I remember, as I flew out for Chris's memorial service, feeling a great upwelling of anger. No one, I thought, should have to go through that kind of experience twice.

The parental cover-up

Yet even then I had little idea what Dad had gone through. Until it happened to me. Until there was no one left to shield me from the realities of giving care to a dying parent.

As long as there's a second parent around, you probably won't have any idea how seriously ill the other parent is. I've heard the same story over and over from others. The more capable parent tends to cover up for the weaker one. As he gets increasingly deaf, she carries on his conversations for him. As she loses her memory, he keeps track of her things, takes her to appointments she's forgotten about. When he becomes incontinent, she cleans up after him – and doesn't tell anyone, because she doesn't want to embarrass him. When she gets dizzy spells and falls, he picks her up, and finds excuses to explain the bruises and scrapes.

I'm astonished at how often the "strong" parent goes first. Your father looked so young, so vigorous, by comparison with others of his age; your mother seemed so competent, so capable. It's the other parent you had worried about. Fortunately, the "strong" parent was still there, and so you didn't have to worry too much. And then suddenly the strong parent dies. In an airport, on a train, in a cancer ward, at a reunion… And suddenly *you're* responsible for the "weak" parent. Because there's no one else.

As long as there's a second parent still around, that parent will assume most of the responsibility. Not because he or she is any more capable than you are. But simply because that's the way parents are. They know that this will be painful for you. They will try to spare you that pain as long as they can.

But when the one parent dies, there is no one left to cover up. And you, the child, become the responsible one.

Causes of complication

How much responsibility you will have to assume depends on a variety of factors.

How many brothers and sisters do you have? As an only child, I couldn't call on anyone else. But others have told me what a relief it is to be able to turn to a sister or a brother for help. You can share the hospital visits.

You can get at least every other evening off. You can talk over the difficult decisions.

How fragmented are your parental families? If your parents are alienated from each other, they can't or won't cover for each other. That means you could become the primary caregiver for each of them. If your spouse's parents have also gone through some kind of bitter separation, one of you – more often the wife than the husband – may end up having to take responsibility for all of them. (Of course, you may end up having to care for a spouse's parent(s), even if they *haven't* gone through a separation.) If you're lucky, they won't all need care at the same time. One woman confessed, in an Internet discussion group, that she was worn out after caring for three declining parents, one after the other: her mother-in-law, her father, her stepmother.

But even if you do end up caring for more than one aging relative, you'll find that each person is a new experience. Some of the tasks may be the same. But the relationship will be different each time.

How far away do you live? Generally, the closest child assumes the primary responsibility. If you're the closest child, you will probably be the one who has to run the errands when your mother can't get to the bank. Other siblings may come around to help your father move into an apartment or a seniors' residence. But you'll have to check out the apartments; you'll have to rent the truck or trailer; you'll have to go around the next morning to help him find his underwear or his wallet. Because the others just aren't there the rest of the time.

How much responsibility have you been officially given? Only the person designated with what's called a "Power of Attorney" can sign checks or contracts; only the executor can process the will and dispense legacies. While it's possible for a parent to name two or more persons for each of these functions, in case of emergency, one person usually ends up carrying most of the responsibility, both before and after the parent's death.

And that can lead to family complications. One husband told me that his wife, the daughter, had to provide most of the care for her senile father. But her father, for reasons now buried somewhere in his mental confusion, had made her brother his attorney and his executor. That brother, the husband fumed, was a semi-competent recluse who never had much practical common sense, who at 45 years old had never left home. She had to badger her brother into making even the simplest decisions.

In another situation, the eldest daughter had official responsibility. She concluded it was best to move their father into an institution where he could receive constant care. She also decided to sell the family home, to pay for this care. The youngest daughter disagreed. She had no authority, but she felt she had the best relationship with their father; she understood best what he would have wanted, were he still capable of saying so.

Family tempests can brew over such disagreements.

And finally, how much care does this parent need? Some parents, even in their declining years, remain relatively independent and self-sufficient right to the end. You won't have to take much direct responsibility for them. At the other extreme, some become so helpless you have to find them full-time care. You won't have to take much direct responsibility for these parents, either. In between are those parents who can't quite cope without your help. That help can become more and more demanding. And exhausting.

Once in a lifetime

Because every aging parent is different, every caring relationship is dif-ferent. That's why I suggest that there's no dress rehearsal for the experience of caring for an aging or dying parent. However it happens, it happens to you that way only once.

Which means, therefore, that when it's your turn, you will come to this particular experience naïve.

And unprepared. Health patterns today make that final decline more unexpected than it used to be. When the Canada Pension Plan was first instituted, according to statistician David Baxter, executive director of the Urban Futures Institute, the average life expectancy was about 68. That meant, he explained to a caregivers' conference in Calgary, that "the Pension Plan only expected to have to pay out benefits for about three years."

Today, life expectancy has risen to about 78. "The Canada Pension Plan isn't in trouble because they're paying too much," Baxter said. "It's because they're paying it out *four times longer* than they expected to!"

Earlier in this century, anyone who made it to 80 was considered long-lived. Today, 80 is almost commonplace. A friend's grandmother lived to 106. She refused to go into a seniors' home until she was 98 – she didn't want to spend her time "with a bunch of old people." When she *did* move, she immediately organized the other seniors, most of them considerably younger than she was, into a choir!

Not only have average life spans increased, average *healthy and usable* life has increased dramatically. Elderly people today stay healthier, longer. Thanks to more universal medical care, new pharmaceutical medications, and improved nutrition, the final decline comes much more precipitously than it used to. A graph of physical health, drawn earlier in this century, would show a long steady slope downwards for most people from middle age on. Each accident, each bout of illness, accelerated that decline a bit more. Today, that graph stays relatively level for most people, like a long plateau, until the final two to five years of life. Many elders stay quite healthy and active into their late 70s and early 80s. They don't get sick as often; they recover from sickness more quickly. Elderly parents can live quite normal lives, almost to the end. But when the end does come, they slide much more quickly towards death.

When you've grown accustomed to their being able to look after themselves, their new dependence on you will come as a massive shock.

Doug Moore

When they couldn't look after themselves

We got my parents into a nursing home when it was clear they couldn't look after themselves anymore. We got a very good place. We were fortunate. It cost us about $2,200 (U.S.) a month for care, which is about two-thirds of what we expected.

Rose and I cleaned up the house that they had lived in for the last 46 years. We thought that they were doing okay when we visited them every three or four months. They put out a little bit of extra effort that concealed how incompetent they were becoming. It took us a while to realize how serious their condition was.

When we cleaned up the house, we filled up a whole table with knickknacks, little souvenirs from this place and that. We asked my mother if any of them had any special value to her, things that she specially wanted to keep in the nursing home. She picked out two things, and that's all. "Everything else can go," she said. But the next day, she couldn't remember saying that. She went back out to the house every day to collect things. She even took things that had already been sold. We asked one day, "Mother, where are the candlesticks?" She had taken them.

We're only beginning to realize now how much she depended on Dad. For example, you can't count on her to come down to dinner properly dressed. One time, she hadn't put a blouse on at all. Dad reminded her of those things before his death. We didn't realize how far she was gone.

Joan*

My third time around

This is my third time around as a caregiver.

When I was 16, I took care of my grandfather. I didn't know much about caring for an older person, but I learned quickly. When I married, he assured me that I first needed to take care of my new husband. To my sorrow, my grandfather died within six months of my marriage. It hurt more than most would have realized.

In 1982, my father-in-law was newly widowed and not able to keep it together. This time we tried the long distance stuff, with hours on the road every weekend. After months of trying, we had to make a big decision, to move. This meant leaving all our friends behind to do what I knew in my heart was right. At first it was easy because his health was not bad. But in 1987 things changed: heart attacks, strokes…My active father-in-law was losing his life and he didn't like it one bit.

In 1992, my second time around ended, leaving me with a better understanding of who I was and who I had become.

In October 1997, I received a phone call that there had been a car accident. My mother was dead and my father was in critical care.

After six weeks in a coma and two weeks in rehab, the doctors announced to me that he would never be able to live unsupervised again. My other siblings were not handling this well, and still are not – denial is a terrible thing. So, in November 1997, they sent this person that looked like my father home with me.

I have a gentle 64-year-old who thinks that everything is fine, but who is unable to do even the most basic care for himself. Every day I see the frustration in his eyes when he realizes that, along with the wife he lost in the car accident that day, he lost so much more.

*From the Internet, Third Age page, no name given.

Diane Forrest

Between friends

I was lucky. I never had to endure my parents diminished or altered, or provide the grueling care so many children must.

My mother was ill, however, for much of my childhood. Perhaps because of that early disconnection, I took longer to leave home than most. A few years after my father's death, I bought an apartment in my mother's building. The move made financial and practical sense. But I was also aware that living "away from home" was much easier when the person who meant "home" to me was just one floor up.

My mother wasn't always the most comfortable person to be around, though, especially once rheumatoid arthritis narrowed the boundaries of her life. She really didn't need me, in any practical sense, other than to open the occasional jar of Dijon.

But because I was close to home, something wonderful happened. My mother and I became something like friends. The fact that she wasn't like other mothers had caused pain during my childhood, but it brought me a lot of pleasure as an adult. What other mother was keen to see the latest Peter Greenaway film? None of my friends' mothers were spending their "declining years" becoming experts on the Bloomsbury Group. I was proud of her and, if she was up to it, it was never hard to find something we both wanted to do.

It's not that there were never bad feelings (we're WASPs, so there were no fights, just tense silence or the occasional bad-tempered outburst) or that we engaged in a lot of deep and animated discussions. What we had was the satisfying companionship of two people who thought pretty much alike about most things.

After a cerebral aneurysm when she was 78, my mother stayed conscious for a day. I had the chance that evening to wish her a good sleep and tell her I loved her. Then she dropped into a two-week coma. After a week, it was clear we would have to let her go.

My three sisters and I each had different ways of saying goodbye. I simply carried on with our usual routine, dropping in to read her a recently published article of mine that included a reference to her, talking about the cruise we never got to take together. I assumed that my mother was doing what she wanted to do – dying – and she didn't need me there to help her or give her permission. But a regular visit and some good talk would be welcome.

Things like that are understood between friends.

෧

TWO

The Shock of Change

No matter how well prepared you think you are for your parent's physical or mental decline, the actual moment you have to take over will come as a surprise. Sensitivity and good communication can ease the transition.

"When my daughter was growing up, I would have sacrificed anything for her, because I wanted her to have a future," Janice Leonard told me. "I make sacrifices for my father, too. But it's different, because there is no future for him."

That's the shattering discovery that comes to all of us, eventually. Your parent is winding down. There is no future. Today is all that the two of you have.

Usually, there are ample signs of your parent's declining health. But the realization of your parent's mortality will still come as a shock. Because you have spent all the rest of your life, up to this time, thinking of your parent as the one who looked after you. And now you're the one looking after your parent.

In the long run, an elderly parent's decline is steady and progressive. And, of course, it is ultimately irreversible, although there are times of improvement and recovery. But the decline is never quite as obvious at the time as it is in hindsight.

The long slide

When I look back over the last decade, there's no doubt about my father's progressive decline. We could see a change in his health every time he came to visit us. When we first moved from Toronto back to British Columbia, Dad used to drive up from Vancouver to our home in the Okanagan Valley. It took him about six hours – an hour or so longer than it took us to cover the same route – but he did it several times a year.

Then he began to split the trip over two days, stopping for an overnight rest along the way.

Then he switched to coming by air. At first, he stepped relatively vigorously off the plane and into the airport terminal. On his final flights, he was a stooped, shuffling old man, being passed by all the other passengers.

But he was still able to travel. And we had trouble believing that the day would come when he could not travel anymore.

About eight years before his death, he got his granddaughter Sharon interested in fly-fishing. She had recently moved from Toronto to Edmonton. She had gone through some employment difficulties: first, a roller-coaster ride of appointments, transfers, promotions, and new responsibilities, followed by an emotionally devastating job loss. Bluntly put, she got fired.

During the nine months or so that it took her to recover confidence in herself, she went fishing several times with my father. For her, it was therapy. For him, it was an enormous relief to find that his fishing gene (if there is such a thing) wasn't going to die out with him.

Thus began an annual bonding experience.

One year, they flew into a remote lake in British Columbia's Anahim plateau, accessible only by float plane, for a week of wilderness fishing. That summer, Dad stood deep in rushing rapids to fish.

The next year, they chartered a boat on the Peace River. Dad waded along the gravel bars.

The year after that, they came to the east branch of the Kettle River, a couple of hours from our home in the Okanagan. One day that week, I went with them – more to provide comic relief than to catch fish. Sharon caught three fish that day. I caught my hat, a snag, the bottom, a tree, and a rock bluff. I also fell in. I slipped on a rock and went in over the top of my hip waders. Until it happened, I would never have believed how heavy waders filled with water can be. If the water had been any deeper, I could have drowned.

But I noticed that Dad didn't wade into the water at all. He fished from the shore. He said, afterwards, that he didn't trust his reflexes in case he slipped. I guess he knew already how heavy water-filled waders can be.

The final year, Dad and Sharon went to one of his favorite fishing rivers, the Skagit, nestled in the mountains by the United States border. Dad didn't even attempt to fish. He found a third person, a friend, to fish with Sharon. He simply watched from the shore while the other two flicked dry flies at their finny foes.

Over those four years, his decline was obvious – from active fishing to passive observer. We could all see the progression. Even so, we didn't believe it could leave him helpless one day.

Sudden transitions

These changes always seem to come with dizzying suddenness, no matter how long they have been developing.

June Vreeswyk was a member of our local church congregation. In her 50s she developed Pick's disease. It acts like Alzheimer's disease, but instead of losing her memory, she lost her words. Her nouns, particularly. She tried to tell me, once, about her childhood in England. "We had animals," she said. "You know, dogs." A blank look spread over her face as she struggled for a word that wouldn't come. "And those other ones, the little ones, like dogs, but not dogs." Her lip quivered. She couldn't remember the word "cats." What's worse, she *knew* she couldn't remember.

She continued to lead the church choir, but more and more vacantly. She could read the music and the words, but she didn't know what they meant anymore. Choir members had to lead her to the music stand, and to turn the score to the opening page.

For two long years, women of the congregation came to spend a morning or afternoon with June, while her husband Peter was at work. Everyone saw how her ability to communicate got steadily worse. She could play cards, but she couldn't name the suits or the numbers. She could walk anywhere, but she couldn't read a road sign. She was a mature woman, who had reverted to the language skills of a two-year-old.

And then – overnight, it seemed – she reverted to the *behavior* of a two-year-old. She became just as rebellious, inquisitive, and unpredictable. She regressed past her toilet training. Yet she still had all her physical strength. Her family had to place her in an institution, where, for her own safety, she had to be kept behind locked doors. Sometimes she had to be physically restrained.

June's progressive decline was obvious to all who knew her. Yet the transition from living at home to living in an institution happened in a few stunningly quick days. Everyone could see it coming; no one realized it would come when it did.

Tipped over the edge

It was the same for us.

We knew Dad couldn't continue taking care of himself too much longer. His health was becoming increasingly precarious. He had had his first heart attack almost 20 years before. For the last ten years, he had depended on an implanted pacemaker, inserted beneath the skin on his chest, to keep his heartbeat regular. Without it, he would certainly have been an invalid; he might well have been dead.

His doctor had also been juggling medications for two competing threats to his life. Dad's already damaged heart couldn't pump blood efficiently out into his arteries and the chronic back-pressure resulted in fluid buildup in his chest. In other words, he had congestive heart failure. At the same time, his kidneys were breaking down. Unfortunately, the diuretics he needed to keep his chest clear damaged his kidneys. And if the doctor eased off on medication to spare Dad's kidneys, his lungs started to drown.

Dad told us, the previous Christmas, "I don't know how much longer they can keep balancing these medications. Sooner or later, they're going to have to make a choice."

We knew. But we always expected it to be "later," not "sooner."

When we took holidays, we always left an emergency number where we could be reached – just in case. Even so, when we came back that January to learn that Dad was in the hospital, having had two heart attacks, it felt as if our world was collapsing around us. Whatever we might have had planned for the coming months, something different had just been propelled to the top of our priority list.

And – to be brutally honest about this – we resented the effect my father's debility had on our lives. In the very short term, we had to call the kennel and extend our dog's stay there. We had to call our neighbor, and ask if she would continue feeding the cats for a few more days. In the longer term, we had to find some way of looking after Dad. We didn't know whether that meant moving him into some kind of institution, hiring help, moving to Vancouver, or moving him to live with us. We *did* know it would affect our time, our income, our savings.

In a booklet called *Parenting Our Parents* (In-Sight Books, 1989), author Doug Manning notes that, "Just as our generation is pushing children out of the nest, our parents are coming home to roost. We had no time for relaxation as a couple between finishing one 'parenting responsibility' and beginning another…Someone has called this the 'sandwich generation.' We are sandwiched between our children and our parents…"

Manning recognizes the powerful emotions this new situation can evoke: "The problem with this timing is that we do not know how we are supposed to feel. If we feel resentment, we tend to think of ourselves as the most ungrateful children on earth..." These feelings don't mean that we don't love our parents, he continues: "These feelings prove we are normal."

His decision

Joan and I knew we would have to get home soon, but we couldn't leave Dad alone. Sharon, our daughter, came to the rescue. Sharon is self-employed. "I'm not busy this month," she said. "I'd consider it an honor and a privilege to be able to help Grandpa for a couple of weeks – until he's back on his feet. "

The three of us checked Dad out of hospital, and moved him back to his apartment.

He was dreadfully weak. He seemed to have regained no strength during his hospital stay. Indeed, the resident told Sharon that Dad's heart function was down to 10 percent. It sounded serious. It was.

Whenever we had stayed with him before, the protocol was clear. This was *his* home; we were *his* guests. If we went out for dinner, he paid. If we stayed in, he cooked. He was in charge. Although he would never put it in these terms, he was "king of the castle."

This time, he didn't even attempt to cook for us. It took all his stamina just to get out of bed in the morning and come out for breakfast. At meals, I had to help him pull his chair up to the table. He toyed with his food, moving the peas around on his plate, raising a forkful of mashed potatoes to his mouth and putting it down again. Two bites of chicken were enough; he chewed them endlessly before managing to swallow them.

Most of the time, he just lay on the living room couch, wrapped in an old housecoat.

The second afternoon, slowly, weakly, Dad rolled over on his side to face us. Joan was embroidering a piece of stitchery; Sharon was working on a quilt square; I may have been aimlessly reading something, trying to keep my mind off gloomy thoughts.

I remember the afternoon as clearly as if it were acid-etched in steel.

"There's something I need to say to you three," Dad said, struggling for the words. "I've come to the conclusion" – he paused for a spasm of coughing brought on by the fluids accumulating in his chest – "that I can't continue here any longer on my own."

And thus the crisis was thrust upon us.

No more time

We had known for years that this moment was coming. But at the same time, we did not want to act precipitately. And we always expected that we would have a bit more time – time to do proper research, time to find the right solution for him.

Now there was no more time.

My interviews with others suggest that this is an almost universal pattern. We always think there's still a bit more time. And when there isn't, people make hasty decisions.

- A mother in Montreal seems to be coping reasonably well in her rented apartment – until she's rushed to hospital with her head split open from a fall. Her son learns that she has been passing out several times a week. The only solution seems to be to bring her to their home in Toronto, to live with them.

- Another mother has her own home. The fire department has to put out a blaze in her kitchen. The only space her daughter can find for her is in Kelowna, three hours away from her friends.

- A father has been getting along reasonably well in Regina, until a small stroke destroys what's left of his coordination and speech. His children unilaterally sell his car and his house, and buy a small house for him in Toronto, closer to them.

Not one person told me, "We saw it coming, and we were well prepared for it."

In my family, Sharon took control. Joan and I couldn't delay our return any longer, so we headed home. We did the five-hour drive up over the Coquihalla Pass – a route that I would get to know very well over the coming months – in a state of shock. I don't recall talking about anything. We were numb.

Sharon worked frantically for a week. She talked to the local director of social services about getting home care, in Dad's apartment. She talked with the nursing orders. "I had to *do* something," she said. "I couldn't just sit around watching him gasp for breath like a dying guppy in an aquarium."

Eventually, as the seriousness of her grandfather's condition became more evident and the feasible options narrowed, she started investigating nursing homes and residences.

A last resort

I didn't know much about nursing homes. What I did know, I didn't like very much. As a journalist, I had visited a number of them, for various reasons. Some felt like vast institutions where stainless steel dollies shuttled along antiseptic halls. Others were converted country homes – small and friendly, but with limited nursing care. A few were appalling warehouses of human misery, where incontinent patients lay helplessly in their own filth until someone got around to cleaning them up.

Back in my high school days, I delivered newspapers to two homes like this. I still remember the darkened living rooms, shades drawn on the windows. In one home, a half-dozen wrinkled old men sat with vacant eyes in overstuffed chairs whose fabric was worn as shiny and thin as the elbows of their jackets. They didn't respond in any way to my presence when I came in with their papers. Even the carpets smelled of urine. The second home was much the same, except that the occupants of the overstuffed chairs were women.

"They're not like that, are they?" I asked Sharon when she told us about her efforts to find a suitable place for my father.

Some were, she admitted. Fortunately, others were clean, bright, and cheerful, with nurses on duty around the clock, and with a good reputation. She chose one of those – Crofton Manor, on West 41st Avenue in Vancouver.

We still don't know if Crofton was the best solution. We will never know if other facilities might have cost less, been more convenient, or offered more personal care. We simply know that, under the circumstances, it was the *only* solution – it was the *only* intermediate care facility that had a vacancy.

Sharon had inspected it. She had walked around, and asked a lot of questions. (For questions you should ask, see Chapter 6.) Every resident had a private room, on the ground floor, with sliding doors that opened out to a garden courtyard. A dining room provided three full meals a day, with several menu choices. Nursing and support staffs were on duty 24 hours a day. And it didn't smell of urine.

Only some of the residents resembled those in the nursing homes I remembered from delivering newspapers, all those years ago. Not all the residents. Some were bright, sharp, with-it, suffering only physical disabilities. But a number sat in the main lounge, blankly watching the television set, but not seeing. On my first visit, I encountered a man dressed in a well-pressed blue suit, complete with tie and gold tie pin, shuffling along the halls, pausing occasionally to examine with mindless intensity a room number, a name plate, a direction sign… On my last visit, he was still doing exactly the same.

Crofton made every effort to keep its residents stimulated. It brought in pianists for concerts, speakers for programs, clergy for worship services. It organized outings and activities. But there's not much you can do for a man who's no longer capable of closing his own hand around the ball for carpet bowling. Or for the woman can no longer see or recognize the target across the room. A terminally cheerful aide has to hold the resident's hand, close it around the ball, direct it, and let the ball go.

No alternatives left

I didn't think Dad would welcome life in such a place. And he didn't. He was unhappy about his loss of independence, the upheaval in his lifestyle, the inevitable regimentation and loss of privacy that happens in even the best of institutions. But he knew he had no alternative. So he accepted Sharon's choice. I can't claim he accepted it with good grace. He was too tired, too weak, to attempt grace. But he didn't argue. He didn't protest. He simply accepted – whatever was coming, whatever was happening to him.

He didn't have any other choice.

When to make a change

Children react differently to a parent's declining health. Some persist in believing that everything is still okay, long after it isn't. Others panic at the first sign of weakness and want the parent to move into some kind of care facility or seniors' apartment.

My personal recommendation is to leave the parent in his or her own accommodation as long as possible. That's how I'd like to be treated when my own time comes.

But don't leave it too late.

One day, Lydia Gabel lived in her own house on the waterfront of Okanagan Lake, a couple of blocks from us. She walked along the lakeshore road every day to collect her mail. She cooked and vacuumed and dusted. The next day, she had a massive stroke, and could do no longer care for herself.

One day, Elizabeth Little lived alone in her own house in Vancouver on the West Coast. She still did her own shopping. She had guests for dinner. She kept her garden up. She seemed, for all practical purposes, to be quite competent on her own. She and her son, who lived back east, had agreed it was time for her to move into her own private apartment in a seniors' complex. She had put her house up for sale; she had accepted an offer.

The next day, she collapsed on the floor of her bedroom. She couldn't get up. And she had one leg trapped beneath her in such a way that it cut off circulation. By the time a friend found her, two days later, her leg had developed gangrene. It couldn't be saved. Nor could she. She was rushed to hospital and put on life support systems. On the advice of a kindly doctor, her family decided to pull the plug.

How do you know when it's time to make the change? That's the hard part – perhaps the impossible part. You can watch a parent's abilities slowly decline. But when does decline turn into incompetence?

Don't assume that your parent will feel the way you do. Your parent may find it hard getting up and down stairs. Or doing the laundry. Or cooking. She may be unable to reach the upper kitchen cupboards anymore. He may not be able to smell the mold behind the toilet. But just because *you* couldn't tolerate those conditions, doesn't mean your parent can't. Or shouldn't.

If there's no physical hazard for parents in continuing to live in the same place, my advice is, leave them there. Minimize the number of losses that aging parents have to experience. Leaving them where they are is usually better than forcing them against their will into a frightening new situation.

And yet…

Our church held two workshops on aging. The first was called, "How we can help our aging parents." The second was called, "How we can help our *children* cope with *their* aging parents" – that is, with *us*, as *we* grow older. As both events progressed, the same message came through to me: *Don't wait too long.* Waiting until change is forced by an accident, a stroke, or an illness, creates multiple problems for everyone. The parent resents the sudden loss of independence. The children are plunged into decisions they're unprepared for. Everything has to get done in crisis mode. It's better for parents to act while the choice is still their own than to wait until there is no choice, and the burden of doing something falls on the children.

Taking the initiative

In fact, that decision sometimes *does* have to fall on the children. The aging parent is either unwilling or unable to make the decision to move into some other housing. And you have to take control.

The parallel comes from child rearing. You teach your children to make responsible decisions about running out into the street, staying out late, associating with friends. You encourage them to choose their own clothes, plan their own careers, develop their own hobbies. But sometimes, as a parent, you still have to step in, to impose your authority. For their own safety.

I overheard a snippet of discussion on the radio, one morning. "If your child goes running out into the traffic," said a man whose name I never caught, "you have an obligation to stop them." Lofty principles about self-determination have to be set aside in life-threatening situations. You can't excuse inaction by saying, "It has to be her choice."

A similar principle applies, I think, with elderly parents. If continuing to drive the car imperils other people's lives, you have to cancel the privilege of driving. If continuing to live alone in the old family home threatens your parent's health, you have to find alternatives. You can't hide behind the excuse, "It has to be their decision," any more than you can let a child keep running out into traffic.

It's more complicated with parents, of course. Psychologist Frank McNair once ventured the opinion, in a casual conversation, that a majority of adults were still working out the parent-child hostilities of their teenage years. So when parents become old and dependent, children may treat those parents as they felt they were treated, many years before. If they were treated with respect and dignity, there's no problem. But if teenaged children were treated with scorn, contempt, despair, or harsh authority, they're likely to mimic that pattern with parents.

Parents, however, no matter how senile or decrepit they become, never seem to forget that they are parents. *Your* parents. They may well resent your attempts to manage them, just as much as you resented your parents attempts to manage you when you were a teenager.

In fact, you may have to use some of the same techniques parents use with teenagers. Plant an idea and let it grow. Express an opinion, without imposing it on your parent. Set limits, within which your parent may have freedom of will. Ask questions, instead of making blanket assertions. Only as a last resort should you be arbitrary and authoritative. When you were a child, you didn't like a parent telling you, "Because I said so!" If you try that response on your parent, she or he won't like it any more than you did.

Above all, try to find the right time. Try to recognize the openings when they occur.

We may have missed an opportunity with Joan's mother. "I wonder if I should be moving into some kind of a home," she said, a few years ago.

"Why?" we asked. "Aren't you happy here?"

"Oh, yes," she replied quickly. Almost too quickly.

"Then stay here," we assured her.

We forgot that the elderly may give the answers they think the other person wants to hear. When I look back, I wonder if Mom was giving us an opening to talk about when she should move, where she should move to, how she should apply. We missed her cue. By the time she was ready to move, she was at the bottom of a two-year waiting list for the only seniors' residence in her community. In the meantime, she found herself increasingly isolated: a neighbor who used to run errands for her had died, another moved away. We waited too long.

If you pay attention, you may be able to avoid making the same mistake. And if you remain sensitive and hone your communication skills, the transition may go more smoothly than you thought possible.

Jeannette Buchholz
It's the helplessness of it all

We tried to get Mum a homemaker, so that she could come back to her own home. We couldn't do it. I'd be quite willing to move into her house to look after her. But I have to work five days a week, plus Saturday mornings. What do we do about her while I'm out?

My husband says, "If you want to take her home, I'll support you. But I have to say to you that I don't think it's best for her or for you." I know that.

How could I provide her with 24-hour care anyway? I can't just leave her alone. We're paying $1,100 a month for her care now, and that's cheap. We can get a homemaker, but at $28 an hour? People say that we can surely get someone for less than that, but if you pay less, what are you getting? If they're goofing off at McDonald's, do I want them goofing off with my mother?

And how long before I burn out, taking care of her the other 16 hours of the day? What would it take out of me? In one sense, she doesn't take much looking after. But it's like having a two-year-old around the house again. You never quite know what she's going to be getting into. The difference with a two-year-old is that you can expect a two-year-old to learn. You can't expect your Mum to learn after two strokes. It can only get worse.

I think it's the helplessness that upsets me most of all. You just can't deal with it, you can't feel that you've accomplished something, gotten it done. There is no resolution. And there won't be one, there really can't be one.

She used to say, years ago, that "when the time comes, I'll have to go into a home." She said, "I'll never be a burden to my daughters." But she didn't act on it in time.

Anonymous*

Ask yourself how you would like to be treated

Treat your parents with the same dignity that you would like to be treated with in about 40 years. I took care of both of my in-laws till they passed away, and although at times they acted like little children and even pouted, I'd just take a deep breath and remember who they were and why they were here.

It's not like they *wanted* to be cared for. They were still young in their minds, only their bodies had aged. It was a frustrating situation for them to find themselves in. Even down to diaper changes. It's so demeaning for them to find themselves depending on others now, especially their children.

You see, they have little choice in the matter. We want them to have the best care – our care. We want to make sure that the last years are spent with those who love them – us. We don't stop to think that all of this is harder on them at their age than it is on us. We will remain, they must go on.

When you look at your parents, don't look at them and just see an old person. Ask yourself how would you like to be treated, how you want to look in your children's eyes, someday. Learn now, for your day is coming too.

The most important ingredient is love.

*From the Internet, Third Age page, no name given.

THREE

A Reversal of Roles

Your parents have taken care of you, most of your life. Now you have to take care of them. It's one of the most profound readjustments you will ever experience.

When you're caring for an aging parent, there's always a fear in the back of your mind that this person could die. But the eventual death of your parent may not be your most traumatic experience. It may be the reversal of roles that takes place.

"It is an awful thing," Hartley Steward wrote in an editorial for Sun Media, "when life comes full cycle and the parent is the child again, in need of precisely the same care he gave to his children most of his life. It is an inexplicably cruel and spiteful turn in the human condition."

It is "an awful thing" because it overturns the habits of your entire lifetime. Whether you have had a warm relationship with your parents or a cool one, they have always been your parents. Even when you're full grown, an adult, those roles don't change. My friend and former business partner Ralph Milton tells about visiting his mother in the hospital, shortly before she died. Ralph bent over her, to tell her how much he loved her; she reached up and adjusted his tie. Joan's mother reminds her to put on a warm coat in winter. Joan rolls her eyes heavenward in despair. But she and I can't resist volunteering advice to our daughter Sharon.

Regardless of our age, the habits of a lifetime cause us to look up to our parents. I remember when I was a child, falling down and scraping my knee. I ran crying to my mother, confident that she could fix it. She did – with some disinfectant, a bandage, and a kiss to make it better.

I also remember walking into my father's study one day, and finding him assembling something that involved red wheels and varnished maple boards. I had no idea what they were or why he seemed a little flustered. Not until some weeks later, at Christmas, did I realize he had been putting together my Christmas present – a wagon from Eaton's mail order. I thought he could fix anything.

Adulation fades, of course. In my teenage years, I discovered he couldn't dismantle and reassemble bicycles better than I could. A few times, I had to rescue electrical repairs he had made to extension cords or living room lamps before they shorted out and either blew a fuse or started a fire. I had to get past adolescence to realize that there was more to life than fixing bicycles and lamp cords.

My mother, to my youthful surprise, turned out to be a superb teacher who knew everything worth knowing about English. Any language skills that I have came from her patient coaching.

My father turned out to have knowledge and understanding that I had not yet learned to value. The summer I graduated from university, I spent working away from home. I read, in some science fiction novel, about a civilization far in the future that turned to a master database, an ancient electronic book, that they kept locked up for times of crisis. It sounded like a parallel to the Bible. I wrote my father, suggesting that the Bible had been written by one genius, many years ago, who had deliberately adopted different pseudonyms to give the impression of the wisdom of a whole community. Dad could have ignored my queries, assuming that I would grow up some day. He didn't. He wrote back –

four pages of single-spaced typing. In those four pages, he introduced me to the whole subject of literary criticism: vocabulary analysis, sentence structure, cultural content, contextual theology, the use of allusion and parable...

I had never realized that these things existed before. Not only that, I had never imagined that *he* knew all these things.

In later years, I discovered how much he knew about philosophy and psychology, about the religions of the East – Hinduism, Islam, and Buddhism – as well as his own Christianity, and even about other disciplines such as quantum physics and mathematics.

Once a child, always a child, I suppose. As a child, I had literally looked up to him. After I grew up, I still looked up to him figuratively.

I suspect most of us, to some extent, find ourselves deferring to a parent's superior wisdom, or power, or experience. The habits of childhood die hard.

In fact, we often defer to our elders even when we know they're wrong. A few years ago, Joan and I visited my relatives in Northern Ireland. My auntie Margie wanted us to see the fabled Mountains of Mourne. My cousin Norah drove, while her mother gave directions. At one crossroads, they got into an argument. Norah wanted to go straight on. "Turn right, Norah!" Auntie Margie commanded. Norah continued to protest. "Turn right, I said!" came Auntie Margie's imperious retort. "I've been around this territory a lot longer than you have!"

Fuming, Norah obeyed. Even though, as it later turned out, she had been correct in wanting to go straight ahead.

You have probably had similar experiences. Even when you disagree with your parents, you yield. Simply because they are your parents.

Transfer of authority

And then one day everything changes. Suddenly, your parents look to you for the answers. You become the responsible one, the competent one, the one who can get things done.

The change may come suddenly, as the result of a stroke or heart attack. More often, it happens gradually, as your parent's mental or physical health sags imperceptibly. It will sneak up on you. You'll keep persuading yourself that your parent is still okay – until one day you realize he or she has become dependent.

Of course, some parents find ways of being dependent on their children most of their lives, manipulating their children to get themselves taken care of. But most, in my experience, do their best to look after themselves, to avoid being a burden to anyone – so much so that often their own children don't realize how difficult their lives have become.

Widows, particularly, manage to conceal their situations. According to Statistics Canada, says Betty Jane Wylie, 74 percent of the elderly population are single women: bereaved, divorced, or never married. Forty percent of them live below the poverty line; it used to be 65 percent, until Stats Can lowered the "Low Income Cut Off" (*Family: An Exploration,* Northstone Publishing, 1997). The picture is much the same in the United States, where 48 percent of elderly women are widowed, as compared to 14 percent of men; and 16 percent of elderly women are impoverished, as compared to 9 percent of men. (U.S. Census Bureau Statistical Brief: "Sixty-five Plus in the United States")

It's one thing to think and talk about being in charge someday. It's quite a different thing to find yourself actually responsible for your parent.

Intellectually, I knew the time had to come. My father had already outlived most of his contemporaries. For that matter, he had outlived many of his students. Joan and I had talked about how to approach him when it was time to give up his car – if not for his own safety, then for the safety of others on the road. We had talked about what might happen when he had to give up his apartment. About finding him institutional care. About helping him dispose of almost a century of accumulated books and letters, furniture and fishing gear, souvenirs and paintings.

But even as we talked, we still thought about him as being in charge. He was the parent; we were the children.

And then, overnight, it seems, the historic roles of a lifetime are reversed. You become the parent; your parent becomes the "child."

Acting as parent to your parent

Biologically, of course, that's nonsense. Biologically, your parent is always your parent; that person cannot become your child. Your mother can never literally become your daughter.

But you probably will, at some point, hold your mother in your arms the way she held you, when you were young. You will feed your father, spoonful by patient spoonful, the way he fed you when you sat in a high chair. You will watch over your parents, rescue them from their mistakes, handle what they're now incapable of handling, just as they did for you many years ago.

There have been times in my life, I confess, when I looked forward to such a reversal. As a teenager, I'm slightly ashamed to admit, I remember thinking, "If Dad were to die, I could wrap Ma around my little finger and get anything I wanted!" Perhaps all teenagers go through such a self-centered phase.

There have also been financially difficult times when I have thought that if I could inherit my parents' savings, I'd be spared a lot of struggle. Perhaps all young adults have such thoughts.

Or perhaps, as Frank McNair suggested, I hadn't outgrown my own teenage relationships with my parents. Those long-forgotten feelings can come boiling up at the most unpredictable times.

When Joan and I had babies, we wiped their bottoms; we cleaned up when they threw up; we got up in the night with them. Those experiences produce a profound bond between parent and child. That bond persists – but now it's the *child* who has to wipe the *parent's* bottom, clean up, get up in the night.

In both cases, these actions can lead to a deep tenderness, an outpouring of love. Or it can lead to anger, hostility, even violence. Granny-bashing and baby-bashing are both facts of life in today's society.

You can't control how your parent behaves in this new situation. But you can change how *you* behave. The more you can treat your parent with respect and dignity – the same way you wanted to be treated when you were younger – the more likely your parent is to respond similarly.

The family battlefield

In some senses, we cannot become adults in our own right until we have cast off the apron strings, until we have rebelled against our parents' dominance in our lives. But for some people, that struggle never ends. Their relationship is a constant battle for supremacy – the parents continuing to assert their former authority, the children permanently rebelling against it.

The reversal of roles itself affects the relationship. Doug Manning's parents moved from Oklahoma to live with him. His father became irritable. He wanted to move back to Oklahoma, with or without his wife. "My father never did adjust," Manning wrote in *Parenting Our Parents*. "In his hometown, he was Tom Manning. In my town he was Doug Manning's father. That may not sound like a great loss, but it hits hard when it happens. In the course of this conflict, I suddenly realized the roles had changed. I was now parent to my father." Then, coining a memorable metaphor, Manning added: "My parents had always been the safety net underneath my high wire, and now I was the net under theirs."

When past relationships between parent and child have been strained, the decline of a parent can be an opportunity for a still-rebellious child to seize supremacy. The child can take over, make decisions, run things; the parent becomes a victim of the war between generations.

Yet I haven't seen much of this kind of exploitation. Perhaps I live in a sheltered world. Perhaps my contacts are not characteristic of the population at large. All I can say is, none of the dozens of offspring I interviewed about their relationship with their parents ever said, "Hah! Now I've got 'em where I want 'em!"

Certainly, I heard about family disagreements. Sometimes parents and children can't get along, sometimes siblings squabble. You can't read Ann Landers or Dear Abby without encountering occasional stories of parents protesting that their children are exploiting them, or a sister fearing that her brother is ripping off their parents. Unfortunately, stress can bring out the worst in people, as well as the best. And no one knows quite as well how to push our buttons, how to make us react irrationally, than members of our own families. What we can cope with from a stranger, we explode over when it comes from a brother or sister.

Open confrontation may be necessary in cases of genuine fraud or abuse. But few of these situations, as far as I have seen, result from greed or avarice. The people involved may have made mistakes, but rarely were they deliberately exploiting a dependent relative.

That doesn't make these conflicts any less painful. But it does offer some hope for reconciliation. David Butler-Jones, a Medical Officer of Health, described to me once how he resolved – and avoided – contract conflicts within his jurisdiction. "We go back to the basics," he explained. "When we can agree on our goals, on providing the best possible health care for our constituents that we can afford, we can almost always work out the details." In the same way, if caregivers genuinely want the best for their aging parents, it's possible to build on those good intentions to achieve agreement.

My own experience suggests that abusive situations are the exception, not the rule. People do care. They care deeply. They try to do what's best.

Solving family disputes

Every situation is different, so I can't tell you who's right or who's wrong if you do find yourself in a family conflict. But I can recommend some tried and tested procedures for working things out in groups.

- *Get people to agree on some rules.* If not these rules, then choose almost any set of rules that will keep you firmly on the subject. Tempers are most likely to flare uncontrollably when family members drag in extraneous concerns, or old wounds from past conflicts. If you can't agree even on this step, try to bring in a facilitator – someone who has some skills but no stake at all in the conflict – to moderate the discussion.

- *Set up an agenda.* An agenda is not a way of railroading the discussion, but of keeping it on track. The agenda should not be any one person's responsibility. It's better if all the siblings (and anyone else involved) can contribute three or four topics. You'll find that these topics often overlap.

- *Discuss only one point at a time.* Discussions are more likely to get out-of-hand when they hop unpredictably from topic to topic.

- *When one person is speaking, listen without interrupting.* The single most important point of these meetings is to hear the viewpoints of others. Listening is not simply a time for marshaling your rebuttal – *listen!* The corollary to this rule is, say what you need to say and stop. Fortunately, most people, uninterrupted, tend to run down in about two minutes.

- *Don't allow anyone to dominate.* That's why, in more formal parliamentary procedure, no one is allowed to speak more than once to a motion. In a family gathering, you don't need to be that restrictive. But if any one person starts throwing his or her weight around, remind them of this rule.

- *Keep talking.* Don't withdraw or sulk. The person who pulls out, who refuses to take part anymore, is just as disruptive as the person who tries to bluster and dominate.

- *Don't start sentences with "you."* Start with "I." "You" sentences often go along with finger-pointing, arm-waving, and angry recriminations. They presume judgment of someone else's actions. Sentences that start "I wish" or "I feel" or even "I'm afraid that" bring the matter back to the personal. They allow for differences of perception.
- *Share responsibilities.* Giving all the responsibilities to one person invites backbiting from the others. One person can deal with the medical staff; another can field calls and communicate with friends and relatives. Another can handle bills, and another deal with lawyers. Even if you have to agree to disagree, you can arrange visiting schedules so that you don't run into each other at the hospital or the nursing home.
- *Know when to give up.* If a relative refuses to cooperate, save your energy for your parent instead of wasting it on feuds and battles.
- *Keep notes.* You don't need formal minutes of a meeting. But just in case that relative accuses you later of some in appropriate actions, it helps to have a written record that on such and such a day, that person refused to help.

Changing communication patterns

The underlying problem of most family disputes is that this is an unprecedented situation. People may have been parents themselves, and reared their own children. But they have never before had the experience of acting as parents to their own parents. The old patterns of deference and rebellion, of submission and competition, continue to get in the way.

The reversal of roles wipes out old patterns of communicating with each other. Just as you had to learn new ways of talking with your children, when they first entered puberty, when they hit high school, when they got jobs or got married, so you have to learn new ways of talking with your parents when they become dependent. "With" them, not "to" them. (In the previous chapter, I suggested some possible communication techniques and patterns.)

Whatever your past pattern of communicating with your parents, it's going to change. I've heard of daughters who talked with their mothers every day, by phone or in person. Other children may have gone weeks or months without contact, as both generations went about their own lives independently. When roles change, you will have to learn new ways to communicate.

You may find it difficult to talk with your parent; you may find your parent responding in uncharacteristic ways. Suggestions get taken as criticisms, offers as obligations, teasing as ridicule. A social worker found that her father had changed from being kind and considerate to being difficult and domineering. But only to her. To everyone else, including the staff in his nursing home, he was the same sweet soul he had always been. It took a while, but eventually she understood why. He was trying to prevent their roles from changing. He had always been in control of his life; now his daughter was. He didn't like it, so he fought back. Whenever she was around, he tried to reassert his authority over her.

For some, the new way of communicating has to be worked out carefully, like walking barefoot on broken glass. You may have to confront silences or hostility. You may have to call in an outside person to facilitate new understandings. For others, the new pattern may emerge fairly easily from the past.

My father and I picked up a pattern that, until then, we would more likely have thought of as *not* communicating. Because we lived some distance apart – for 25 years with most of a continent between us – we tended to see each other only a few times a year. So our conversations were fairly intense. We talked about what had been happening to each of us, what projects we were working on, what ideas we were wrestling with. We dug out the information we had stored over the last weeks or months, things we thought would interest the other. After a day or so of this, we ran out of current topics. But by then it was time for one or the other of us to leave, to return home.

In Dad's debility, we slipped back almost 40 years. Back then, while I was still living at home, we were more likely to sit in the living room, reading silently, occasionally interrupting the other's concentration to discuss some thought that rose off the pages.

Those silences became the pattern of communication after Dad was diminished by his heart attacks.

He didn't have the stamina for sustained conversation and I was one of the few people he didn't feel *obligated* to talk with. He could just lie back and rest. By the same token, I was, I suspect, one of the few who felt comfortable just going into his room and sitting quietly. I sat in a chair in his room, and read a book or magazine – or sometimes typed on my laptop computer. We shared occasional sentences, back and forth.

Yet it was through our apparently fragmented discussions – a sentence here, a sentence there, a thought dropped and later picked up – that we began to talk with each other about the things that really mattered to both of us, things we had never discussed before. His death. His funeral. His last wishes for himself, his health care, his possessions…

It was a precious time. I miss it.

Wendy Smallman

My mother is driving me crazy

I have had ongoing problems with my stepmother for years.

I am an only child. My mother died when I was ten. Father and I emigrated to Canada from England that same year. Father remarried three years later. He died a year ago. Mother is driving me crazy.

I had a heated argument via phone with her last night. She has always been very sensitive. I learned right from the start of her marriage to my father that I had better censor anything I might say to her. As a result, I have always been extremely cautious around her.

At times in my late teenage years, she accused me of "talking to all my friends about her," or of "giving her only the old spoons when I set the table." These accusations were so sudden, and violent, that I would almost faint when they happened. However, these moments seemed to lessen with time, and after I left home I was spared more of them.

She possesses what I call a social personality. She can talk to anybody, anytime. (Whereas I, without the extroverted influence of my husband, would by now be a poetry-writing recluse in some cabin in the woods.) Most people really like her; few have seen her dark side.

Since my father died she has tried, by innuendo and veiled reference, to drive me away. She accuses me of "never liking her." After a year of vilification, I'm beginning to think that this is true. God knows, I have tried my best, but it has never been good enough for her. She is a vast, bottomless well of neediness. She keeps taking digs at me, insinuating that I am in touch with other relatives far more than I am with her (and am, therefore, marginalizing her).

I can only conclude that she has some unfinished business within her own family relationships down the long corridors of time, and that I am the wrong person in the wrong place.

❧

Bobbie*

The end of her adult life

My mother was beginning to have severe problems due to dementia. Even impaired, she had many reasons why she couldn't and wouldn't leave the house she had lived in for 37 years. She just wanted us to go away and leave her alone.

Mom had always been a sweet, intelligent, and wonderful lady. But one day she had just had enough. She told us she was sorry she had had any of us, and that she might just as well take the "soothing syrup" and be done with it! We were devastated! Our mother was threatening us with suicide! We spent the afternoon going through her things to convince ourselves that there was no bottle of "soothing syrup" (a codeine concoction used in the early 1900s).

My sisters and I decided to split up the summer, each of us staying with her for a month.

After about a month, she threw the "soothing syrup" gig at me again. But by this time, I was tired, hot, and missing my husband. I told her to go ahead, that when I put her obituary in the newspaper, I would say that she had taken the soothing syrup rather than go to our home for the summer, and that all her neighbors would know. It stopped her short. She never mentioned the soothing syrup again. About a week later she announced to me that she thought it would be a good idea if she went with us to California for the rest of the summer.

That was the point where she ended her adult life and started returning to her childhood. We took over at that point, and she never again even tried to regain control.

---

*From the Internet, *Third Age* page, no name given.

Carolyn Terry

Bossed around by his children

At the end of his life, Dad was more alone than he had been for years, because Mom wasn't with him mentally. At the same time, we, his kids, were busy telling him instead of listening. We all had solutions. Mostly we told him what he should make Mom do, and he tried to tell us he couldn't make Mom do anything. He hated being bossed around by his children.

Mom wouldn't let her homecare worker give her any personal care. She didn't want help bathing or washing her hair. She was in danger of losing her worker, because Medicare wouldn't pay for someone to chat with her for an hour.

I remember my brother telling Mom that she had to allow her worker to help her, and telling Dad that he had to make Mom accept help. Dad kept saying, "I can't make her do anything she doesn't want to do." He seemed tense, wound up tight, and very frustrated that he couldn't make us understand.

Then there was a fuss because Mom lost her hearing aid and Dad couldn't find it anywhere. My brother tried to impress on my Dad how much better off Mom would be if she wore her hearing aid. We would get her a new one, and Dad was to see that she didn't lose it.

All through my life, my Dad was very even-tempered. But when he was at home with her and Mom was blind, forgetful, and stubborn, he was sometimes very grouchy. Yet if I tried to listen to what he was saying, he would calm right down.

Terry Samuel

Walking on thin ice

My father was convicted a number of years ago of abuse involving family members, and served his time. Following that he has been virtually shunned by most of our family. Following his release on parole, he lived for about 18 months with my wife and me.

He now lives in a retirement home for seniors and gets plenty of attention for all his needs. He's 89 and still driving his car (a warning to all on the road). He has an indefatigable sense of humor, and he is enjoyed by many in the parish and community. He sings in his church choir (when he can manage to huff and puff his way up into the chancel) and loves to be at the center of the action.

His parole officer told him that since his parole is finished, he is now free to contact people (victims) he was formerly forbidden to contact. The parole officer, seeing his anxiety, suggested he write a letter of apology to one person in particular, who has been seriously distressed by the whole story.

Knowing the situation, I agreed with the suggestion, but said I'd like to feel things out with those relatives before actually sending the letter. I suggested to Dad that he might write the letter and hold it until the right time.

This brings up the whole dilemma of family relationships, though. My brother is in a difficult position, since his wife would find untenable any thought of my dad communicating with her daughter (one of the victims). My brother, therefore, finds himself in an awkward "in-between" situation.

This is only a microcosm of the larger world of tension and tentative relationships that characterize our family these years. A lot of us – more or less – walk on thin ice, trying to be proactive in terms of healing, but also respectful of peoples' pain and need for more time.

FOUR

Caring for Your Aging Parent

Caring for an aging parent involves a multitude of difficult care choices and decisions. And it is made more complicated by two factors – living close by, and living far away.

From what I've seen, if you live close to your parent, you're more likely to suffer frustration, and less likely to suffer from guilt. If you live at some distance from your parent, the situation is reversed – you're more likely to suffer guilt, but perhaps have less daily frustration.

The perils of living close

A friend of ours was astonished to discover that her 85-pound mother, who has osteoporosis and a bad back, had somehow managed to rearrange all the furniture in the den – including the 250-pound sofabed.

"Why didn't you call us, Mum?" our friend protested. We only live five minutes away, you know."

"I didn't want to bother you, dear," her mother replied.

Distraught, our friend pleaded with her mother not to take such risks again. Her mother agreed. And, indeed, on her next visit, our friend found all the furniture in the house still in place, as promised. But the garage had been thoroughly cleaned out, including a stack of heavy boxes filled with books.

Even with their disabilities, many parents still want to be independent. They don't want to have to turn to their kids every time something needs doing. So, perversely, they may store up tasks that you, as the nearby child, could easily have done, until your brother who lives 350 miles away comes for his twice-a-year visit.

Or else your parent may go to the opposite extreme. You may become your parent's primary source of help. For everything, from picking up the mail to putting out the garbage. You may not be particularly skilled at plumbing, or at starting stalled cars. But since you're accessible, you're the first person your parent calls when the toilet tank cracks, or the car quits. One daughter I heard of was getting five or more calls a day from her mother.

Over and over, the people I interviewed shook their heads sadly, but not angrily, about their parents' idiosyncrasies. One called about a burned-out light bulb. "I'd fix it myself," she said, "but you told me not to climb on any ladders." Another called for help stopping his newspaper delivery, while he was vacationing. He could cope with flying to Arizona, but the newspaper's automated messaging system was too much for him: "Press 1 for account information; press 2 to cancel; press 3 for a change of address…"

At the same time, they hate admitting that they can't cope. In the role reversal that happens with aging parents, they want your approval, just the way you once sought their approval for things you had done. So you probably will *not* get a call to say that your father had a dizzy spell and fell over while he was getting his breakfast. Or that your mother just sent $5,000 to a man who convinced her she had inherited a condominium in Florida from an uncle she didn't know she had, but it would cost $5,000 to clear the administrative paperwork before she could take possession. You probably won't get the call because they're embarrassed about these things, and would really prefer that you didn't know about them.

You *will* hear about them, of course. Eventually. When it's too late to do anything more than hope your parent has learned something from the experience.

Jeannette Buchholz runs our village post office. It's just one block away from her mother's house. Her mother didn't seem capable of recognizing that Jeannette was at work. "We had to take mother's license away a few years ago," Jeannette told me. "It wasn't safe for her to drive anymore. She came here, to the Post Office, while I was looking after other customers, and insisted she needed to go to renew her license. I said I didn't want to discuss it here. I said I'd come over after work and we could talk about it then. But she insisted it had to be done – right now! She stamped her foot, like a child having a tantrum. So I finally said, 'No, Mum, I'm *not* going to re-license you. It's not safe.' She went away quite angry. But when I went over later, she never brought it up again. I think it was a bit of a relief to her. I took the responsibility away from her. Now she could use me as an excuse."

The problem with being the child who lives close by is that it's difficult to get away, to have your own life. The day our local church sponsored a community dinner, one of our friends phoned up. "Are there any extra tickets?" she pleaded. "I bought ours, but I forgot about my mother. She'll be hurt if we leave her out. Can I bring her along?"

The problems of living away

Conversely, if you live far away, you may or may not hear about the light bulb and the newspaper. More likely, your parent will turn to a neighbor or a friend for help with these inconveniences. You may be family, but you're not available.

If there's no friend or neighbor available, your parent is likely to pick someone at random from the Yellow Pages of the telephone directory. Most of these trades are honest, in my experience. A few of them are even kindly – they'll respond to your parent's obvious need by doing more than is expected of them. They'll not only fix the toilet tank, they'll also repair a dripping tap, in exchange for nothing more than a cup of tea. Unfortunately, an equally small percentage of these people are ruthless and unscrupulous. They are predators, who treat confused and uncertain elderly people as easy prey. Our local newspaper carried a story of a woman in a fairly small house in Vernon, a city just north of us, who paid over $25,000 to have her roof reshingled and her eavestroughs replaced. Each repair led to another repair, and another…while the invoices kept growing.

By the time you hear about these disasters, it's often too late.

About all you can do is insist – even to the extent of getting righteously angry – that your parent deal only with firms that they *know* have been around for a long time. These firms may not give any better service. But if they have roots in the community, they're less likely to skip town after cashing your parent's check.

Joan's mother bought an expensive hearing aid from a sales representative who came through her town every couple of months. When it failed to work properly, she tried to contact the sales rep – only to learn that he had headed south of the border with a lot of customers' cash. He wasn't likely to come back to do repairs or adjustments. Fortunately, the parent company, the manufacturer of the hearing aid, stood behind their product and did the repairs at no charge. But Joan had to bring the hearing aid back to Kelowna, a day's drive across five mountain passes, to start that process. There was no one, literally no one, in her hometown that Mom could turn to for help with a very technical problem.

If you don't live close to your parent, you will only hear about these difficulties occasionally. And after the fact, of course. Your parents may have lived through the Depression; if not, they were born in or influenced by the Depression and War years. They learned the value of a penny very early. A dollar still feels like a lot of money. Given that mindset, many don't like to "waste" money on long distance telephone calls. Joan learned about the hearing aid problem only after her telephone calls went unanswered for several days; her mother couldn't hear the telephone ringing.

The effects of a mobile society

We run into these problems because we live in a mobile society.

There was a time, not that many generations ago, when parents lived close to their children. Or, more accurately, the children never moved away. The children lived in the same town, often worked in the family firm, or took over the family farm. When the parents grew old, the children moved back into the family home. They became the permanent, unpaid, caregivers for their parents.

In earlier generations, moves were usually prompted by land grants. Joan's grandparents moved from Ohio to try farming the dustbowl of southern Alberta. In the same way, my ancestors left Scotland in 1827 to homestead in southern Ontario.

In our times, the lure has been jobs. California, the eastern seaboard of the United States, southern Ontario, parts of Alberta, have boomed. People hungry for affluent lifestyles have flocked to where the jobs are. During the 1960s and 1970s, corporations moved their employees almost randomly. Where we lived for 25 years in Don Mills, now part of Toronto, IBM was a major employer. In those years, IBM relocated its employees so often, we joked that IBM stood for "I've Been Moved."

Mobility put us in Toronto. When we got married, we first lived about ten miles from my parents (though about 400 from hers). I got a promotion, which meant moving to Prince Rupert, about as far north as you can go along the coast of British Columbia without running into Alaska. That put us about 1000 miles by road from both sets of parents. My next job took us to Toronto, most of the way across the continent.

These moves were good for us economically. But they separated us from our parents by more than just miles. Our son Stephen felt more grief over the death of one of our cats than over the death of Joan's father. "I hardly knew Grandpa," he shrugged. "But Sylvester slept on my bed."

It was partly the recognition that neither Joan's mother nor my father had much time left that prompted us to move back to B.C. in 1993.

We knew, intuitively, that they would not move and come to us; the older people get, the less likely they are to move. Children move away from their parents; parents themselves rarely move away from their children. Some do, of course. Enough make that choice to justify the existence of retirement havens like Victoria or Kelowna, and to keep a lot of recreational vehicle outfits in business. But they're a minority, according to David Baxter, a prominent social statistician. Mobility belongs to younger age groups. So does home purchasing. As people grow older, they pay off their mortgages; they own their own homes; they stay put.

If seniors *do* move, Baxter says, they usually don't do it for climate or recreation. Most seniors move for only two main reasons. In the period soon after retirement, they may move to be closer to their family, especially their grandchildren. In their closing years, they will move into some kind of care facility.

The caring choices

When your parent is no longer capable of living alone, the range of options open to you may seem limitless. The choices are complicated by terminology. If you're unfamiliar with the terms, what's the difference between a "homemaker" and a "home care worker"? Between "intermediate care" and "extended care"? Between a "residence" and a "villa"?

It seems to me, after reading enough books on elder care to cure insomnia for the rest of my life, that your choices boil down to three:

- To have your parent live with you.
- To arrange for care in your parent's home.
- To move your parent into an institution.

Most of us react emotionally against the third option – an institution. As Jean Clayton noted in her book *The Tiny Red Bathing Suit of Mr. July* (Wood Lake Books, 1997), "Few people come to continuing care institutions willingly…For many people, admission to continuing care somehow signifies the end of life. And they are right – it is the end of life as they have known it." Statistics and anecdotal evidence both indicate that most people decline rapidly after being admitted to an institution.

And yet institutional care is, for most elderly persons, ultimately inevitable. Somewhere around 80 percent of people today die in hospitals, which are institutions. Some go in for only their final few days; others may need to spend months, or longer, in a palliative care ward.

More commonly, parents spend some of their time in an intermediate or extended care facility. Again, definitions vary. As I understand and use the term, extended care is for people who pretty much need assistance around the clock; intermediate care means that the residents can look after themselves at least part of the time. They can get to the bathroom at night on their own, for example. They're usually mobile, to some extent. They can usually feed themselves. An intermediate care facility will count out pills; it will not administer intravenous medication or provide continual bedside care.

When your parent's condition requires more services than the care facility can provide, he or she will usually be transferred to a hospital. In practice, they may be shuffled back and forth quite often. Anne or Grace, two of the day nurses at Crofton, usually called me to inform me about problems Dad had had during the night. I gathered up some clothes, my laptop computer, a few files, a few books, and hit the road. After the first couple of times, packing turned into a familiar routine. It only took a few minutes before I was on my way.

Steps in making a decision

When you're considering the possibilities for your parent, here are some suggestions to help you make the right choice.

- *First, consult.* If your parent is currently in the hospital, talk to the hospital's discharge staff. They have to deal with these questions over and over. Talk with your parent's doctor. If you live in the same area as your parent, talk with your own doctor too. Find out how serious they consider your parent's condition. How much help does he or she need? How often? If they require help with medication or therapy, a visiting nurse or therapist, a few times a day or week, may be enough. More severe disabilities may call for part-time or full-time assistance, or may mean moving into an institution. But don't assume, too quickly, that an institution is your only alternative.

Doctors can also help you figure out the steps you'll have to take, and the people you'll have to talk to, to get help.

- **Second, explore.** Talk to the director of your local social services agency, whatever it's called. Find out what kind of assistance is available. Are there visiting nurses' associations? Are there homemakers, who can come in to handle burdensome housework or errands? Are there volunteer associations and agencies, such as Meals on Wheels, who can provide nutrition? Ask who pays for these services. Some may be free, some subsidized, and some frighteningly expensive.

  One woman living on the East Coast told me that around-the-clock nursing care for her mother had cost her $8,000 a month. "Thank God she died in two months," she added tersely. It wasn't a callous comment – there were tears in her eyes as she said it.

  Again, don't leap to conclusions about care possibilities. Explore as many possible solutions as you can.

- **Third, interview.** By telephone, initially. If you're considering hiring in-home help, study the guide in Appendix 1. Don't accept the first applicant – remember you're putting your parent's life in this person's hands. (And if that isn't enough to make you cautious, remember that you could also be putting your parent's bequests in their hands.) If you're working through an agency, don't just talk to a supervisor or administrator. Also ask your doctors about this group. Ask the social services director. Ask the Better Business Bureau.

  If you decide you have to move your parent into an institution, interview their representative as rigorously as you would an individual applicant. Ask, for example, how many registered nurses they have on during the night. How many people each nurse is responsible for. How long it takes to respond to a call for help. What choice of meals and menus they offer.

Whether you're interviewing an individual or an institution, ask for references. And follow up on them. References may not protect you from an outright swindle – in that case, the person you contact will be part of the scam – but most people are painfully honest about an applicant's strengths and weaknesses.

- *Finally, visit.* Go and see the institution. Walk through it. Use your eyes, your ears, your nose. Observe how the residents are treated, how clean the halls are, how meals are served, and what's on the bulletin boards. Ask to see their Mission Statement, or Guiding Principles. See whether it's posted where all staff are constantly reminded of it, or hidden in a supervisor's office. Get rates in writing. Check whether there's a place for residents to get themselves tea or coffee (and perhaps a cookie).

If you're considering hiring an individual, try to visit a previous client. What sort of condition did the applicant leave her room in? Under what circumstances did he leave?

If you're looking for part-time assistance, you may be able to go with the applicant to other calls. How does this person relate to others? It is difficult for anyone – applicant or client – to maintain a false front while giving or receiving treatment.

But having done all that, in the end, you still have to make a choice. And if you have to act quickly, you may have to accept slightly less than ideal conditions.

Other forms of housing

Beyond intermediate or extended care facilities, there are other options.

Consider senior citizens' residences, for example. They all offer some benefits over the traditional single family home – if they didn't, they wouldn't exist – but those benefits vary widely.

The simplest form of seniors' housing is a small subdivision restricted to owners over a specified age – often 55, but sometimes 60 or 65 – and often referred to as an "adult community." The houses or townhouses may be more compact. They're usually on one floor, with rooms and appliances set up for easy use. Many are fully wheelchair accessible. Lots are smaller, and there's usually some provision for having the complex take care of gardening when the owner or tenant is away. Some of these communities also offer security, either by gates that restrict access, or by regular patrols.

When aging parents can no longer cope with a regular house and garden, but don't require constant care, these communities might provide an interim step that allows them to retain their independence without it becoming a burden.

Then there are seniors' apartments. Some are like a regular apartment building, but with a minimum age limit. Your parent would do his or her own cooking, cleaning, etc. Others offer more services. One that we checked into had full apartments, with one to three bedrooms, and small kitchens. But it also had a dining room, where residents could enjoy full meals. And its own hairdressing salon, for residents who had difficulty getting out. And a nursing station, with a nurse on call around the clock.

Yet another possibility, sometimes called "Supported Living Apartments," blurs the line between independent living and institutional care. Aging parents have their own apartments, their own furniture, their own decor. They live privately. But they can have three meals per day provided, and have their housekeeping and laundry done for them. Nurses, physiotherapists, and aides make regular visits, and provide some levels of medical care.

Obviously, the more services you contract for, the higher the monthly cost. Generally, though, these units are still cheaper than full institutional care.

The least expensive options

But suppose your aging parent can't afford any of these institutional options. Then you have only two choices left: provide care in your parent's present home, or move your parent in with you.

Care in the current home is more feasible than it used to be. Governments everywhere are slowly recognizing that it costs a lot less financially to subsidize people in their homes than to subsidize institutions. It's also better for the people they subsidize, emotionally and physically.

And you might be surprised at what's available. For example, in the city nearest me, which has a population of no more than 100,000 people, a non profit society called the Care & Share Foundation advertises the following services:

- **Home Helpers** – Light housekeeping, Cooking, Companionship, Shopping, Errands, Respite, and Live-in Support.
- **Home Sitters** – A free service to enhance your home's salability or care for your home while you are away for three or more months.
- **Home Handyman** – Professional work for all your repairs, maintenance, and renovations, big or small.
- **Home Hair Care** – Complete hair care in your home by certified hair stylists.

Joan's mother lives in a much smaller town, of barely 10,000 people. She and her two sisters – all three well over 80 years old – have "homemakers" paid for by government social services. (If you have to pay privately for these services, rates can run as high as $30 an hour.) How much time they get each week depends on their level of disability. Joan's mother, with all four limbs still functioning, has a homemaker for two hours a week. One of her sisters had one arm disabled by a stroke; she got four hours a week. The third sister, legally blind, also handicapped by a stroke, receives around six hours a week.

Nurses also visit. Some are privately paid; some, depending on where you live, may be covered by government plans. They will dispense medication, give therapy, change dressings, and – if they consider it necessary – call in an ambulance or a medical doctor.

It's even possible to have 24-hour nursing care in the home. But, as I indicated earlier, the costs can be astronomical.

If all your parent needs is someone available in case of emergencies, you might consider renting a room to a student, some other elderly but still able-bodied person, or a struggling young couple willing to exchange companionship and some help around the house for a place to live. The care won't be as professional as you'd get from a nurse or a homemaker, but it will certainly be less expensive. It will probably be better emotionally, because your parent won't feel like an invalid who needs help. It may even turn into a warm and rewarding friendship.

In your own home

The last alternative is to move your parent in with you. In *Family: An Exploration,* Betty Jane Wylie cites figures indicating that 11 percent of older women, over age 65, live with other relatives.

In some ways, this is by far the best alternative. Your parent spends his or her final years physically close to those who are also emotionally closest – you and your family. No one has to travel far to visit. Grandchildren can come to a familiar environment. Aging parents are not isolated by visiting hours, as they are in hospitals or nursing homes. Perhaps most important, those parents can still be treated as individuals in their own right. They bring with them memories and associations that make them unique and valued.

Parents living in your home are not just cogs in an institutional machine. Contrast Jean Clayton's description of life in many care facilities:

Residents may be given medication without discussion…Their choice of meals may be limited or nonexistent. If they cannot feed themselves, they may be fed too quickly by too-busy staff, so that eating becomes stressful rather than pleasurable. They have to go to bed and get up at the convenience of others…They may have little or no influence on the temperature of their room, and must depend on the kindness and patience of others for almost everything. Having a cup of tea when the mood strikes, or getting up to watch TV and have buttered toast when they can't fall asleep, becomes a wild and unlikely dream. *(The Tiny Red Bathing Suit of Mr. July)*

Having your parent live with you could be one of the best things that has ever happened to either of you. It can give you the gift of time to get to know each other in ways that were not possible when you were a teenager rebelling against parental authority, or when you were a young adult beginning to forge your own career. "You get to fill in more squares in the quilt of life," Anita Baker suggested poetically. Anita encouraged her mother to write out the untold stories of her life, and those stories formed the basis for some memorable conversations. "She had 88 good years," Anita said, looking back, "and only two not-so-good ones. That's a pretty good average."

And yet, for some people, having an elderly parent in the home can be soul destroying. Either they're underfoot constantly, or you have to keep checking on them. If you want to go out, you have to get someone to come and sit with your parent – and it's a lot harder to find a sitter for an old person with Alzheimer's than for a child. You have to plan meals for a digestion that no longer works as efficiently as it used to. And you may still struggle with parent/child competition.

Beyond that, the continuing burden of responsibility can wear you down. Down on the Taylor family farm in southern Ontario, my father's cousin got Alzheimer's disease. His mind went completely. He had been a noted local historian. The last time I saw him, he sat by a window, methodically tearing pages out of old books – his history books – and shredding each page into tiny scraps that he placed in neat piles on the table in front of him. His wife cared for him. Day and night. One winter night, totally exhausted, she fell asleep. He got out of bed, and wandered out into a blizzard. Searchers found him the next day, frozen to death.

How would you feel, if he had been your father, and you had brought him into your home to take care of him?

My colleague and friend at Wood Lake Books, Alan Whitmore, had a different experience with Alzheimer's. To give his mother a break, Alan moved his father temporarily into a home, and took his mother down to Mexico for two weeks. "She was a basket case for the first week," he told me. "I had no idea what caring for him was taking out of her until we got her away from it all." When they returned, Alan moved his father into a home, permanently.

If you're thinking about moving a parent into your home, remember that your life matters too. You can't become a doormat.

The problems of elder abuse

Unless you take care of yourself, you're more likely to commit what's called "elder abuse." Or, less politely, "granny bashing." That often results from losing your patience. You've had one too many demands on your time and your energy. Caring for your parent is running up bills you can't afford. Then your parent makes an unreasonable demand. Or drops something. Or just forgets something – for the hundredth time. And something inside you snaps. You start yelling, screaming, maybe even hitting your parent.

I'm not talking here about systematic violence and exploitation. Yes, there are instances of children ruthlessly ripping off their helpless parents, bleeding their bank accounts dry and then abandoning them. Or of using physical force to subdue and control their parents, until they cower in terror. The staff in hospital emergency rooms have learned to ask the same kinds of questions when elderly persons come in with a succession of broken arms, cracked ribs, black eyes, or split lips that they would ask about children.

To quote Betty Jane Wylie again:

No one, not even the experts, can accurately determine the extent of the physical abuse of elderly family members. Older people don't just fall between the cracks of the social system: there *is* no system, at least, none that they are connected to. They're not out in the community where their bruises can be *seen*. In fact, they're probably confined to the house (or sometimes locked in a room)…Also, they're reluctant to report violence, or too frail, or too fearful of reprisals…

There is, unfortunately, a kind of mentality that craves power over others. The weaker the other person is, the easier it is to exercise that power. Children and elders become the favorite prey of this kind of person. He – occasionally she – delights in inflicting pain. Being able to make others suffer becomes a self-justifying proof of this kind of person's superiority.

But I doubt if that description fits you. You probably wouldn't be reading this book if it did. You're reading this because you genuinely want a better relationship with your parent. You want to help in any way you can.

But sometimes things just get overwhelming. And they're more likely to get that way if you have an aging and increasingly frail parent living with you all the time in your own home. You deserve a life too.

Unflattering feelings

No matter how you choose to care for your parent – in your home, in his or her home, in an institution – you will almost certainly find yourself experiencing emotions you're not particularly proud of. You may hesitate to mention those emotions, even to your spouse, for fear others will think less of you.

In the interviews I did, most people looked sheepish at some point, and said something like, "You know, it's weird, but there were times when I wished she'd just die and get it over with." These are normal feelings. They become abnormal only if you start acting on them. At one extreme, to hasten your parent's death, actively or by neglect. At the other extreme, to cut yourself off, to abandon your parent to someone else's not-so-tender care.

In February, a month after my father was first hospitalized with those two heart attacks, he almost died. Joan and I began wondering how well equipped we were, emotionally, to handle any more close calls. His debility almost killed him; it almost destroyed us.

And we knew it would happen again. We just didn't know when. The possibility hung over our daily lives like a vulture circling in the breeze. We lived with a constant, pervasive sense of dread. Or perhaps of futility. Things might *get* better, but they couldn't *stay* better. The end was inevitable. No matter what we did in the meantime.

That can lead to a temptation to do nothing. To simply let the end come. And that could well be a reasonable conclusion, if we operated by logic. But we don't. We operate in a complex mix that includes logic, emotion, beliefs and convictions, sentiment, social standards, family upbringing… And therefore, each time the nurse called to say that my father had had another crisis, I hit the road again.

Between January and August, I made nine trips to Vancouver, most of them on short notice. After his death, I made four more. Each trip amounted to more than 600 miles of driving. Over the year, that amounted to over 8,000 miles of unplanned travel.

As well as being emotionally taxing, these visits were financially stressful. The travel alone cost money. Meals grabbed in the hospital cafeteria, long distance telephone calls, extra pajamas and underwear to purchase for Dad – all these added up. The trips also stole time from writing and editing projects I was contracted to finish.

Dad offered to pay for my costs. I told him not to worry about it. If we had been harder up financially, I might not have been so generous. But in reality, there were three not-very-flattering reasons for refusing his offer:

a) I didn't want to seem to exploit him;

b) I didn't expect him to live very long; and

c) when he died, I expected to recover my costs from his money anyway.

Employment blues

In many ways, I was fortunate. Being self-employed and partly retired, I didn't have to justify my repeated absences to a boss, even an understanding and sympathetic boss. As an only child, there was no one else with whom I could share some of these responsibilities. If I had been conventionally employed, I don't know what I would have done.

For most children of aging parents, employment adds another whole level of stress. You cannot take a week off every time there's an emergency call. You cannot walk off the assembly line every time your parent falls; you cannot let a parent monopolize the telephone lines at your office. You have responsibilities to your employer, your colleagues, and your staff, as well as to your parent.

There are no easy answers. Nor do most books offer solutions. They tend to assume that you will conform to your company's regulations, and that's that.

It doesn't have to be. During the years when I was part-owner of Wood Lake Books, our management meetings debated the granting of compassionate leave. We were prepared to allow time off with pay, when a parent died. But what if parents were just sick? What if they got sick again, and again…? How much leave – with or without pay – could we permit? Eventually, we developed an unwritten guideline: if caring for that parent mattered more than keeping the job, we would grant as much leave as necessary. It was a circular definition – getting leave depended on taking it, before you knew you had permission. As a policy, it certainly wasn't cut and dried. It may not even have been particularly compassionate. But it reflected reality.

There will be times when the well-being of your parent matters more than anything else, even your job. How much absence your employer will tolerate, and on what terms, you will never know in advance. Some bosses are astonishingly tolerant; some keep their hearts in a deep-freeze. Some will grant leave with pay, some without pay, and some won't grant it at all. My experience says that most will bend as far as they dare, provided they don't feel that you're taking advantage of them.

So take time to talk with your employer. Explain the situation. See what you can work out together.

Guilt

Whatever you do about caring for an aging or dying parent, you'll almost certainly end up with some feelings of guilt. Guilt, because you let your employer down. Guilt, because caring for your parent strained relationships with your spouse or children. Guilt, because you didn't do enough for your parent. Or even guilt, because you felt relief rather than remorse when the end finally came.

Guilt is a particularly pervasive and destructive feeling. Most religions are good at fostering guilt. I once joked that the churches should organize a travel agency called "Guilt Trips."

There were times when, I admit, I almost hoped my father would die. And not always for reasons I like to dwell on. I simply got tired of taking second place in my own life. I got tired of having my plans and projects repeatedly interrupted. I got tired of not having time to service our cars, of little things going wrong. And I confess it occurred to me, driving past the new car showrooms, that when we inherited his money we might be able to replace our clunky five-year-old Mazda 4x4 van with a shiny new Audi A6 Avant wagon with its marvelous Quattro drive… (We live on a very steep hill. Without all-wheel drive, a snowfall can trap us for days.)

Then I felt guilty, even having such thoughts.

But guilt is such a useless emotion.

I felt enormously guilty, for example, that I wasn't at my father's bedside when he eventually died. Two days before, my father had been taken to hospital with angina. I'd received the usual phone call from the nurse at Crofton Manor: "Mr. Taylor? I'm sorry, but we had to send your father to hospital this morning…" It took me a day to penetrate the labyrinth of the hospital's telephone extensions to talk to Dad. I was getting frantic. I was committed to being writer-in-residence at a church training center outside Regina, and I couldn't get through to him. When I finally reached him, he sounded dreadful. He was demoralized at returning to hospital, after two months of relatively good health. But the ward nurse told me he was doing fine. His doctor insisted he was just there for observation. He'd be going back to his room at Crofton Manor in a day or two. And Dad himself told me quite emphatically, "You go! I'll be fine."

I believed them. So I flew to Regina, where 20 people had registered for the event. The program director, Jim Von Riesen, had just helped me lug my suitcases up to my room when his son called up the stairs, "Jim Taylor? You're supposed to call your wife. She says it's urgent!"

I knew, immediately, what that meant. Dad had died. My call to Joan merely confirmed the details. Dad had had a visitor from his church congregation in the morning. She had left, promising to come back after lunch. He ate some lunch, lay back for a nap… By the time the visitor returned, he was gone.

In spite of six months of advance warning, I was still unprepared for the sudden reality of his death. And although it sounds silly to say it now, I didn't know whether I should cancel the writing event or try to continue with it.

Fortunately, Jim Von Riesen rescued me. He had suffered a family bereavement himself, a year before. He called the airline, got me a flight out that afternoon, and hustled me back to the airport. I caught the last flight of the afternoon with less than five minutes to spare. The airline staff had my ticket waiting – I grabbed it as I rushed past to the plane. The flight attendants pulled the door shut behind me.

But I spent weeks feeling guilty that Dad had died alone. I was haunted by the thought that he might have opened his eyes, at the last minute, looked for a loving presence with him, and felt abandoned. I felt that I should have canceled the writing program and gone to Vancouver.

But I would have felt equally guilty if I had canceled the writing event and ruined the plans for 20 people and their households, and Dad had *not* died.

Whatever I did had equal opportunity of being wrong, of inducing guilt. It was a lose/lose situation.

Everyone I have talked to about caring for an aging parent has shared similar experiences. We rationalize our decisions. We assure ourselves that we did all that we could have done, that we had no choice about the things we did or didn't do. But we still can't help feeling guilty.

Nothing I can say in this book will change that reality. Only you will know whether you did all you could. If you did, your feelings of guilt will pass. (If you didn't, maybe you *should* feel guilty.) At some point, you will be able to sense your parent saying to you, "Well done, son. Thank you, dear."

Elizabeth Barker

A helpless feeling, so far away

My mother lives in Vancouver; we live a day's drive away. She received a phone call late on a Friday evening from someone claiming to be from Revenue Canada. He said that she owed a lot of money in income taxes. She is new at dealing with financial affairs, and she feels confused. She is proud of her new found independence and her ability to deal with affairs that formerly my father would not let her deal with. But she has never done income taxes.

She was given a phone number to confirm this call and information. But the number, of course, was unavailable until Monday. She told me of the strange call on Saturday.

It sounded to me like a potential phone scam. I called "Phonebusters" – a 1-800 line with the Ontario Provincial Police. They said they had about 34 "hits" on their database of Revenue Canada scams.

To make a long story short, though, it seems that the call to my mother was legitimate. Revenue Canada *does* make calls to clients up to 11:00 p.m. Eastern time. An employee at Revenue Canada said they now make phone calls before they send out letters because they think it is more personal.

Fortunately, my mother did not give out account numbers and had not yet sent any money. But how do we protect our elderly from phone scams if Revenue Canada employs the same practices?

My mother had also told this caller that her husband was in the hospital. So someone could now know that my mother was alone in her house – and this person had her phone number and address. If it had been a scam, I would be really worried. Yet my mother would have been incensed if I had called the police or seemed in any way to be interfering in her affairs.

If my mother knew what anxiety this had caused me, she would likely not tell me next time she gets a suspicious phone call. And if one suspicious phone call turns out to be legitimate, then the elderly may assume *all* calls are okay. The fact that the elderly "trust" enables scammers to succeed.

I have a helpless feeling being so far away.

Anonymous*

My mother refuses to leave her home

My mother is now totally blind. My first thought was that there is no way she can take care of herself or provide for her daily care.

I work for the Department of Human Services. I have investigated many situations very similar to my mother's. I have removed persons from their home to facilities where their needs would be met. I have talked to many caregivers and insisted that they provide more care for their parent, to insure their safety, even if it goes against their parent's wishes. Many told me, "Mom refuses to listen to me. I know she can't stay by herself, but she refuses to leave her home. I can't do anything about it."

Now my own mother refuses to leave her home. She too states that she can do better in her own familiar environment than anywhere else. After numerous chats with my brothers, who live in different states, I knew that I had to deal with this.

I began applying for every service I could find to assist her. I was fortunate to find Visual Services. The worker quickly came to Mother's home. She gave her hope of remaining independent. This worker has been blind since age 13. She allowed my mother to voice her fears and concerns, and to grieve over the loss of her eyesight. She arranged for many services offered by her agency, including a support group which I also attend. My mother was thrilled over the support group – before we could never get her to join in any activity.

She now has book tapes to listen to, raised dots attached to her stove, and other innovative devices for the blind. She is eagerly looking forward to receiving her talking watch. She also has a wrist band for an SOS service in case she has an emergency.

We have also obtained services who come into her home five days a week to assist her with her activities of daily living. I continue to assist her with her finances. Not only is my mother continuing to reside in her own home but my fears and concerns have been greatly reduced. Both Mother and I realize that the day will come when other arrangements will have to be made, but until then, with the assistance of these fine agencies, her wish to remain in her home has been answered.

At the same time, I have learned to be more open-minded and have gained compassion and understanding for my clientele and their caregivers.

*From the Internet, *Third Age* page, no name given.

Bobbie*

We interviewed over 60 homes

We interviewed over 60 care homes up and down the California coast. They were either private homes or gigantic warehouses of misery. Finally, we found a 16-bed home so full of love we almost cried for joy. There were others there like my mother. One woman in particular sought her out, and the two of them had the same animated conversation over and over, to the satisfaction of both. She was in a world we could not enter, and she no longer saw ours. Mother was happy there and they loved her.

When she finally was no longer able to feed herself, we had to transfer her to a nursing home and the hunt began again.

We thought we had chosen a good one, but it turned out to be a horror. We took her out immediately and found a smaller facility where most of the staff had been employed for at least five years, many of them more than ten years – an important factor to look for. Although Mother was unable to communicate with us, nor did she really know who we were, in this home she was always smiling, unlike when she was in the previous one.

We were fortunate, but we never took it for granted. We kept making daily and sometimes twice daily visits. We made friends with the staff and gave our praise. It is a two-way street.

She was there seven months before she died peacefully in her sleep.

*From the Internet, *Third Age* page, no name given.

૨૱

FIVE

Grieving the Losses

Increasing age brings increasing losses for the elderly, and for those who care for them. Each loss becomes a potential cause of grief.

There's something you have to recognize. Your parent's personality is going to change. This seems to be – to a greater or lesser extent – a universal experience. The changes may be massive, when a normally gentle person becomes violent. Or they may be nothing more than a ruggedly independent person becoming dependent, even helpless.

The change can be hard to deal with. "My mother doesn't like anything anymore," lamented one daughter. "She complains about the home she's in, about the food, about how often we visit her. She thinks everyone's trying to cheat her."

On the other hand, it can be a relief. "My wife's mother was – I don't think I'm being unfair in saying this – a really crabby woman," one man confessed. "But since her stroke, she's much easier to get along with. She thinks everything is just wonderful."

Some of these changes result from medications. Some result from physiological effects – strokes, Alzheimer's, Parkinson's, arteriosclerosis…

But a great many result simply from their changed circumstances. Simply put, they're grieving. So are you. And your parent may well be feeling that *your* personality has also changed, as you have assumed new responsibilities.

The symptoms of grief

Every grief results from some kind of a loss. And at this time in your lives, both you and your parent are experiencing a great many losses.

Grief has many facets. I spent an entire book exploring grief. (The book was originally published by Wood Lake Books as *Surviving Death*, in 1993. Northstone Publishing republished it in 1996 as *Letters to Stephen.*) I won't attempt to repeat all of that here. But the most common symptoms deserve some mention.

I call them symptoms, because that seems to me a more appropriate word than the "stages" commonly referred to. Dr. Elisabeth Kübler-Ross gave us "stages," in her pioneering work *On Death and Dying*. Until then, no one had done any serious study of dying people. They were simply banished to nursing homes, hospitals, or back rooms. Dying was dying – that was that.

Kübler-Ross showed us that people faced with terminal illness went through five definable stages:
- shock and denial,
- anger,
- bargaining,
- depression,
- and eventually acceptance.

Unfortunately, many people reading her books misunderstood her point. They thought of the stages as clear and distinct, like grades in school. First you deal with shock and denial; then with anger; and so on.

It's true that there is a progression. Hardly anyone can get to acceptance, for example, without first having to pass through denial. But it's also true that anger can, and often does, flare up in the midst of depression. Bargaining – the kind of situation where a lung cancer victim says, "God, if you can get me through this, I promise I'll never smoke another cigarette" – often starts at the same time as the shock of diagnosis, and may never end.

So I prefer to talk about symptoms rather than stages. These symptoms are feelings. Some of them, like sudden irrational anger, are easier to recognize than others. But if you can recognize the feelings, you may be able to better identify what's happening to you. And why.

For example, I recall driving home from work one day in the early 1980s, when I said to myself, "I feel so depressed." My job as managing editor of *The United Church Observer* was coming to an end. I loved that job – in many ways, I still consider it the best job I ever had. I had given myself to it heart and soul. But a change in management had made my position untenable. For the first time in weeks, I had named the feeling that caused me to drag myself through the day, every day. But as soon as I named it, it was relatively easy to recognize the cause. I had been kidding myself that I didn't really mind, that I was being noble and self-sacrificing in resigning without being forced out. It was a lie. The sudden awareness of drowning in depression made me admit the depth of my feelings of loss. Only when I had begun to recognize what was happening to me, could I begin to visualize an eventual acceptance of my new situation.

Most people going through grief think that no one else understands, that no one else has ever experienced these emotions before. And it's true – no one else has had either that identical experience, or those identical feelings. But everyone who has grieved has discovered at least some of these symptoms. As you read about them, you may recognize some of your own or your parent's reactions.

- *Numbness.* You go through the motions of each day, but feel nothing. You're in shock, a protective reaction of your body to protect you from total breakdown. That's what Joan and I felt as we drove away from Vancouver the first time, after leaving my father behind with Sharon.

- A *brittle competence.* Some people comment, during this time, that they actually feel filled with a kind of manic clarity. You may not feel confident, but you do feel that you're coping pretty well with a totally new situation. Sharon felt this as she chased around Vancouver finding an intermediate care facility for her grandfather to move into.

- *Denial.* You're convinced that your parent, your aunt, your uncle, will recover. You persuade yourself this is just a temporary setback. Things will revert to their familiar pattern again. Even after Dad moved into Crofton Manor, I left everything in his apartment just as it had been – just in case he ever came back to it.

- *Anger.* Irrational rage flares unexpectedly. The extent of the anger may bear little correlation to the cause. If another driver cut in front of me on the road, I wanted to smash into his rear bumper to teach him a lesson. (I didn't.) More pertinently, during one of Dad's hospital stays, the newspaper I thought I had canceled kept arriving at his apartment door on Sunday mornings. Not any other day. Just on Sunday. I tore a strip off a subscription clerk who was not, in any sense, at fault.

- *Wallowing.* Painful as past memories are, you need to dwell in them. It's like bathing a wound – it hurts, but it helps. It's an element in your own healing. As you live through your memories, over and over – as you tell them to others or to yourself – you do two things. First, your mind gradually begins to make sense of what seems like a senseless series of events. Second, you gradually distance yourself from your pain. You turn memories into mere memories of memories.

- *Mood swings.* One moment you're feeling quite normal, the next you're torn apart by tears. One moment you're laughing, the next sobbing. It happens for no apparent cause: a casual question, an old clipping in a scrapbook, a tune on the radio. My father tended to burst unpredictably into tears at any expression of sentiment. I could visit Dad in his room at Crofton Manor, and go "home" to his apartment feeling fine. I'd sit down to read, or watch television, and suddenly be aware that he was *not* sitting across from me in his favorite easy chair. And I dissolved…

- *Depression.* Utter weariness is the other side of anger. You feel drained of all energy. You just want to sleep. Or hide. After Dad's death, for example, I thought I was coping just fine. I was not broken up. I was not devastated. Then I caught myself going back to bed again after breakfast. In the same way, Dad reacted to his loss of independence and privacy by spending several months doing little more than sleeping. He roused himself only when he had visitors.

- *Apathy.* Or maybe despair. You feel you can't change anything. Nothing you do will bring back the past, or make the future any easier. So you just don't care anymore. About anything. Not money. Not friends. Not commitments. It's another way of protecting yourself. Nothing matters. The care facility Sharon found for her grandfather cost almost $4,000 a month – so what?

- *Guilt.* When you can't vent your anger against the real cause – which may well include your aging parent, your siblings, the doctors or nurses – you may turn the anger inward and start to blame yourself. Phrases like "If only…" or "I wish I had…" are sure signs of guilt. I wished I had been able to share Dad's passion for fly-fishing with him. It was an irrational wish. We had shared many other enthusiasms together: painting, travel, theology, philosophy, history… And we had, in fact, gone fishing together several times. Nevertheless, I caught myself saying, "If only I had made time to go on more fishing trips with him."

Losses for you

Any of these symptoms may show up as a result of any loss. And during the role reversal, when a parent becomes dependent on a child, there are a great many losses involved. For both the parent, and the child.

For you as the child, of course, there's the constant fear that your parent, the person who has known you as long as you have been alive, may die. No, *will* die.

Psychologists have a name for that fear. They call it "anticipatory grieving." One of the early books on this subject, *Grief, Dying, and Death* by T. Rando (Research Press, 1984) says, "In the anticipation of a future loss, a form of normal grief can occur. It is termed anticipatory grief." A similar book, *Grief Counseling and Grief Therapy* by J. W. Worden, (Springer Publishing, 1982) says, "The term anticipatory grief refers to grieving that occurs prior to the actual loss."

But Victoria, British Columbia, grief counselor and psychologist Nancy Reeves claims there is no such thing. "I've worked as a clinical psychologist specializing in grief, loss, and trauma for 16 years, and I rarely see anticipatory grief," she asserted flatly in an article she wrote for me, in the clergy journal *pmc: the Practice of Ministry in Canada*.

She used the example of a young wife, sitting by her terminally ill husband's bed. "Try telling that young wife...that she has not yet had an actual loss, because death has not yet occurred. If you really listen to her, she will tell you somewhat forcefully that she is grieving *actual present losses*. They have more impact on her life than her husband's future death. These losses include becoming a single parent, having no sexual or other contact, financial problems resulting from his illness and the amount of time she has had to take off work, a sense of being betrayed by the medical profession because their family doctor refused to send her husband for tests until the cancer had spread...and so on and so on."

From her work, and from my own experience, I extract a principle: you cannot grieve what hasn't happened yet. You can try to imagine how you will feel – but you will never know how you will feel until it actually happens. What you grieve are your present losses.

So you may grieve, for example, the disruptions that your parent's disability create in your normal activities.

• *Telephone calls.* You may find yourself getting telephone calls several times a day, sometimes about the same subject. Your parent can't remember that she called you about the same thing half an hour before – but she can always remember your telephone number, somehow.

- *Visiting.* If you live close to your parent, visiting can turn into a chore. "I used to go up every Monday, Wednesday, and Friday to visit Mum in King City," Carolynn Honor told me. "It took two to three hours each time. I wondered why I was doing it, because most of the time she didn't even know that I was there. I dreaded going up there. I went because I was her daughter, not because I wanted to go. Many times, I would get partway there, and have to pull over to the side of the road and admit to myself, 'I just can't do this.' Sometimes, I really couldn't, and I turned around and came home again."

- *Travel.* As I noted in the last chapter, responding to emergency calls in a distant city can consume massive amounts of time. At one point that stressful spring, Joan calculated that – between my trips to Vancouver and business trips to eastern Canada – I had been away from home more days than I had been at home.

- *Family tensions.* Your spouse, your children, may resent the amount of time you have to spend caring for your parent. Most people today already lead what Thoreau called "lives of quiet desperation," as they juggle endlessly conflicting demands on their time. Throw an aging parent into the mix, and potential conflicts quickly escalate.

- *Financial pressures.* When an aging parent requires specialized care, expenses pile up faster than a snowdrift in a blizzard. Nursing care, ambulances, medication, specialists' appointments – even with medical insurance, there are always extra costs. Even if the parent has the funds to cover such charges, they will quickly eat into any anticipated inheritance. And if the parent doesn't have the funds, they can drive the children deeply into debt.

Loss of an image

But beyond these practical losses, there's the loss of an image you have held in your mind since you were a child – the image of your parent as bigger and stronger than you. I was far more devastated, emotionally, by my father's helplessness than by his eventual death.

It hit me hardest the day we moved him from his apartment into Crofton Manor.

It was a temporary room, until his own room had been cleaned and repainted. The lawn outside his sliding glass door was lush and green, though no leaves had yet come out on the cherry tree. Inside the room, the furniture was sparse and institutional: a single hospital bed, a comfortable chair, a small dresser, a narrow little closet. We hung a few shirts, some slacks, a couple of sports jackets, on the rack in the closet. We put his supply of socks, of underwear, in the dresser. We set his shaving kit on the counter in the bathroom.

He lay back on the bed, propped up with pillows. He looked shrunken, as if his bones and skin had imploded. His clothes hung loosely on him. Out of courtesy and convention, he tried to carry on a conversation with us. He couldn't sustain it. Speaking took too much effort. He left his sentences unfinished and sank back into silence.

His friend, fishing partner, and former minister, Alan Reynolds, came to visit. For a few moments, there was a flicker of warmth in Dad's eyes, a trace of animation in his voice. They shook hands. And Dad lay back, exhausted by even that little effort.

When Alan rose to leave, I went out with him. In the safety of the hall, I burst into tears. Alan wrapped his large arms around me. "It's hard," he said. "It's hard to see him like that."

For the first time, that first day in Crofton Manor, I knew I was going to lose him. And I was not prepared for that loss.

Losses for your parent

For your parent, on the other hand, death may not necessarily be the most serious loss. Often, the elderly are quite ready to go – indeed, they *want* to go – but it's the other losses that destroy their spirit.

One of Joan's aunts, for example, had a couple of strokes. Each one disabled her a little more. Her third stroke left her collapsed on the floor, while her sink overflowed onto her. The puddle got to be almost two inches deep before her homemaker arrived and found her there. Both her left arm and her left leg were paralyzed. She could feel nothing in them. She said later, from her hospital bed, "If I could have made myself roll over, I would have tried to drown myself in two inches of water."

She feared helplessness and disability more than death itself.

Others will find their loss of independence hardest to accept. Many of our parents survived at least part of the Great Depression, World War II, the Korean War, perhaps the Vietnam War. They learned to look after themselves. To accept help now – to *have* to accept help – feels like a betrayal of everything they have been so far. And they hate being on the receiving end of charity.

About a year before my father had to go into institutional care, we became increasingly concerned that he might not be getting adequate nutrition from the meals he cooked for himself. We suggested that he could have at least one good meal each week, delivered through Meals on Wheels or some equivalent. It's one of the few times I saw my father angry. He had been, in his prime, about 5'8" tall, though he had shrunk somewhat with age. But as he listened to our suggestion, he drew himself up straighter. His eyes flashed. "I will *not*," he snapped, "accept charity! I can look after myself!"

Loss of mobility, too. For most elderly people, a car is more than a means of getting around. It symbolizes their continuing independence. Even if it's cheaper for them to take taxis, they keep the car. It is, after their health and money, their primary concern. Allen Dobbs, Professor Emeritus of Psychology and Medicine at the University of Alberta, and president of DriveABLE Testing Inc., a research center for studying the driving abilities of seniors, told a workshop in Calgary that some senior citizens' organizations have banned any discussion of cars or driving during the last half hour of their meetings. It's too hot a topic. Once opened, it's impossible to shut down on time!

My father bought a new car at the age of 88. His driver's license was valid until the year 2000. He drove himself to church, to meetings, to gatherings of friends. Rather to our surprise, he did not drive himself to the hospital after his heart attacks. He didn't drive much at night, though – and then only on familiar routes.

That's also characteristic of elders, according to Allen Dobbs. As their night vision and their reflexes deteriorate, our parents feel less and less comfortable driving at night, or on unfamiliar roads. So they just don't drive anymore in those circumstances.

Even after he was hospitalized, my father hung on to his car. More accurately, he hung on to the *illusion* of the car, the comfort that the car gave him. He wanted it moved up to the parking garage at Crofton Manor – just in case. On one of my business trips to the east, I chose to fly out of and back to Vancouver, so that I could spend a few days with Dad at either end. I told him when I would be returning from Toronto. He sat slumped in his easy chair in his room, wrapped to the chin in housecoat and blankets, with little energy to do more than raise his head. But he said, as he had so many times before: "I suppose I could drive out to the airport to meet you."

Loss of freedom can be devastating for many seniors when they move into an institution. They can no longer eat when they feel like it. Meals are served on a schedule, at the same time, every day. My father accepted the schedule of Crofton Manor, because he knew it was necessary. But he didn't like it. His own routines were equally regular. But they were his own – he could change them if he chose to. In his apartment, he got up when he felt like it, even if his alarm *did* go off at the same time every morning. But now a nurse's aide came around to wake him in time for breakfast. He used to have a bath every night. Now he had his bath scheduled for him – half an hour every Tuesday and Friday evening. I was talking with him on the telephone one of those Tuesday evenings. He cut me off abruptly: "I have to go. The woman has come to give me my bath."

Loss of privacy. The aide *gave* him a bath. She was there; she scrubbed him; she toweled him down after it. Fifteen minutes before supper, every evening, another aide popped his door open and called to him: "Dinner time, Mr. Taylor!" He had to get used to people walking in on him at any time, without warning.

Loss of choice

The late Karen Carpenter sang, in one of her recordings, "Bless the beasts and the children…for they have no choice." She might have added, "and the elderly." Age often becomes a winding down of choices. My mother-in-law broke her hip ten years ago. She recovered the use of her hip, but she never recovered her self-confidence. A widow, she still lives in the simple two-bedroom house she has owned since 1973. But where once she stumped vigorously about its rooms, she now shuffles slowly and cautiously. She used to walk two blocks to the supermarket and shopping center; now she rarely goes out at all. Not even in summer, and certainly never in winter. She's afraid of falling, of injuring herself again.

As eyes and ears and muscles weaken, elderly parents have less and less freedom to do what they want. Their choices narrow down.

The number of losses the elderly experience challenges my imagination. Loss of physical strength: tasks that used to be easy become increasingly difficult, even impossible. Loss of sight: you try to read, and it becomes too hard to process the words. Loss of hearing: conversations that you used to love become a drone. Words pop in and out of focus, but you don't catch enough of them in-between to keep track of what people are saying. You wish they'd slow down…

A friend gave us a clue to what was happening with Dad. "Is your father having trouble hearing you?" she asked.

"Yeah," I admitted. "I have to speak slowly, and much more loudly."

"It's not that his hearing has gone," she explained. "It's that he can't process what he's hearing fast enough. So he thinks it's your problem. He thinks you must be talking too fast, or not clearly enough."

That also helped me understand why he stopped reading. Dad loved books. But for months after his illness knocked the stamina out of him, he read next to nothing. We moved a bookcase into his room at Crofton Manor. He told me which books he wanted to have with him. But whenever I went into that room, I found the books still left exactly as I had left them. At first, I thought he was having some difficulty seeing. If he did pick up a book or magazine, he peered at the pages as if his glasses were dirty or badly scratched. When I had a chance, I checked his glasses. I couldn't tell if they were the right prescription, but they certainly weren't scratched or dirty.

"Reading makes me tired," he explained. Processing thoughts required energy that he didn't have anymore.

Becoming a burden

Then there's loss of control. Dad could cope with his loss of health, his weakness. But he found it terribly difficult to admit that he couldn't manage his own affairs anymore. He couldn't keep his checkbook balanced. Attempting to gather his charitable donation receipts for his income tax return reduced him to helpless tears.

Dad was quite ready to die. He was not ready to be a burden.

Some of these losses, as I said, are far more devastating – for the person involved, and for those who love them – than actual death.

One of our responsibilities as caregiving children is to minimize those losses. Our parents need to retain the power to make as many choices as possible. So that they don't feel useless, or unwanted. The less they have to grieve, the fewer internal conflicts they have to reconcile, the more they can move towards reconciliation, with others and with the end of life itself.

One thing we did right with my father was to leave as many decisions as possible in his own hands. He didn't have much choice about moving to Crofton Manor – although it was, initially, his own decision that he couldn't stay in his apartment. And he was not physically capable of doing the research to find a care facility for himself. But almost everything else was his decision, even if we had to do the work for him. He chose the furniture that would go into his permanent room. He chose the pictures that would hang on his walls. He chose the clothes that would hang in his closet.

We could have insisted that he give up his car. Others have arbitrarily forced their aging fathers or mothers to give up their cars, to cancel their drivers' licenses. We didn't – with some trepidation, I admit. We weren't worried that he would kill himself in an accident – after 75 years of driving, he could anticipate most situations. (We did learn not to create new and unpredictable situations, like asking him a question while he approached a stop sign, or sending him to an unfamiliar location at night.) But we worried that he might kill or injure someone else.

Nevertheless, we didn't insist that he give up his car. That too had to be his choice.

The dignity of making decisions

In the same way, the decision to sell his apartment came from him, not from us. "I'm not going to live through the fall," he told me in May. "I'd like you to have the apartment to stay in, when you come down to Vancouver. But maybe we could sell it and have a long closing date so you can continue to use it while I'm alive."

I had to make contact with a real estate agent. I chose Lee Davison, a woman who had once lived in the same building, and who had a parking space next to his. Dad liked Lee, and had confidence in her. I got the process started. But from there on he handled the negotiations. Lee visited him at Crofton Manor to discuss offers. He signed the papers. He accepted or rejected the offers.

Admittedly, he often called me for advice. I told him, once, that he didn't need to. "You know what you want, Dad," I protested. "Even if you've given me Power of Attorney, it's still your decision, not mine."

"I know," he agreed. Then he chuckled: "But you're a good excuse. You let me take a little longer to make up my mind."

Loss of mental powers

Loss of mental functions may be one of the hardest losses to cope with, for both the parent and the child. Hartley Steward wrote about his father, at 83: "Like many others his age, he is fighting to retain his hold on the world. He closes his eyes and puts his head in his big hands and he strains with all his might to catch himself in time and place. Then he looks up. Shakes his head and smiles in embarrassment. 'Why doesn't someone just take my hand and tell me where I am?' he asks us."

An aging friend of ours lost his short-term memory in a stroke. He could still have an animated discussion, probing and challenging my theories about anything. But he'd tell me, "In 15 minutes, we could be having this conversation all over again, because I won't remember it." Then he had a second stroke. He can't carry a conversation anymore. He just sits, and beams, and lets his wife do the talking. Physically, he's the same man I knew. Mentally, he's a stranger.

And he knows it.

With loss of memory also goes a loss of personality. So much of who we are is bound up with who we were, what we have done. Hartley Steward tried to express his father's situation: "How do you imagine a future when you have no past?…At the moment of realization, it must surely seem that you're at the gates of hell."

When memory goes, we have to start building a new relationship with a parent. And it's a strange kind of relationship. Only the memories and loyalties still held by one of the two persons involved in that relationship provide motivation. The other party doesn't know, and doesn't care.

"My mother doesn't know who I am, most of the time," Elaine Towgood says. "Cathy, her nurse for the last three years, goes out of the room, and Mum says, 'Do I know that woman?'

"Our son Paul was driving her up to the Okanagan one Christmas. She looked at him partway up, and said, 'You're a very nice young man. Have I met your parents?'"

This is one aspect of loss that I never had to face. Aside from a very short period when my father suffered delusions resulting from medication, he remained lucid right to the end. Even right at the end, when his brain was working so slowly that he spoke in slow motion, when I had to repeat a simple question three times for him to grasp it, his brain was at least still working.

I was extremely fortunate. But one or two conversations during those few days gave me a a brief glimpse of the pain and confusion caused when a parent's mind gives up the struggle. I found that experience at least as upsetting as Dad's physical debility.

A different person

Dad had been checked into hospital with a cough that the nurses at Crofton Manor couldn't control. The resident at the hospital decided to try Demerol. It worked, in one sense. It eased Dad's cough. It got him through the crisis, and gave him a chance to return to something closer to good health.

But it also had some very negative effects. Demerol is renowned for causing hallucinations. In younger people, these hallucinations fade fairly quickly as their kidneys flush the chemicals out of their circulatory systems. But Dad's kidneys were in as bad shape as his heart. As a consequence, the Demerol kept circulating through his system for days.

The first symptom was that Dad's hands started twitching. He kept plucking at his sheets, his blankets. Occasionally, he looked down at his twitching hand, as if surprised. He suddenly reached out for something in front of him. His fingers closed over nothing. He shook his head, puzzled. "I thought there was a plate right there," he said.

"A plate?"

"Yes. With my dinner on it."

He also began hallucinating. I came to his hospital room one morning to find him sitting up in bed. He looked alert for the first time in several weeks.

"I'm glad to see you're sitting up today," I said. "How long have you been up?"

"Since I came back," he wheezed cheerfully.

For the next half hour, I tried to make sense of an incredible tale of a parade through the streets of Vancouver, a television broadcast, a Communist plot, a police investigation, and mind-control experiments.

My father was normally a very rational man. Even in his delusions, he could be utterly rational about an irrational situation. When I tried to catch him out in his facts, to bring him back to reality, he looked puzzled and shook his head. "It's all because of this medication I've been on," he apologized. "What's it called?"

"Demerol, Dad."

"That's right. It turns out that there are two kinds of it." He spoke as if lecturing obtuse students. "One of them is benign, developed as a pain-killer and sedative. The other was specifically developed to produce disorientation and hallucinations. And that's what they've been giving me."

"You sound as though it was a deliberate act."

"It was. They wanted to… what's the word I'm looking for?"

"Affect? Manipulate?"

He looked pleased. "Manipulate – that's it. To manipulate my mental state. The two nurses who were here yesterday were part of it. Olga and… and…"

"Sarah was on last night."

"Yes, Sarah. The little one." At least he had her description right. Then he shifted from recognizable fact into extravagant fantasy without blinking an eyelid: "Olga and Sarah have gone back to Russia."

"They went off shift," I corrected him.

"They're not here today, are they?" he concluded triumphantly, as if their absence proved his point.

Later that morning, I offered to remove, from the bridge of his nose, one of those expander strips to flare his nostrils a bit and ease his breathing. He recoiled. "No," he insisted. "The police officer told me not to remove anything that might be evidence."

"But I put that on you, myself," I protested.

"He said not to remove anything," Dad continued, and added, with irrefutable logic: "It's anything."

Not what he would do

Another time, abruptly, he whipped his glasses off. "Here!" he insisted urgently. "Put my glasses on!"

"What for?"

"So you can hear them talking to me." The tone of his voice said that it made perfect sense to him, even if it didn't to me.

I put his glasses on. He's long-sighted; I'm short-sighted. "They make everything fuzzy," I reported.

"Of course they do," he replied. "They're the wrong prescription for you. But can you hear them?"

I shook my head. "I don't hear anything that I couldn't hear before."

"You can't hear those trees outside there?" He gestured at the two fir trees outside the window.

"No. Do you?"

"When I've got my glasses on. They're shouting at each other, beating each other with their branches in the storm."

I glanced out the window. "Dad, there's no storm. They're perfectly still."

"Well, of course, I can't see that when you're wearing my glasses."

"Can you *hear* them while I'm wearing your glasses?"

"No." I wondered if I had found a chink in his illusions. But I hadn't reckoned on his ingenuity: "The metal ear pieces must be some kind of an antenna, picking up the signals for my hearing aid."

"You don't wear a hearing aid."

"They must have implanted one."

"Dad, I can see into your ears. There is no hearing aid there."

His own logic triumphed again: "Of course you can't see it. I told you – it was implanted."

I found the whole conversation so disturbing that I had to go out into the hall, to get away from him for a while. My father was still my father, even when his body wasn't working. But he was not the same person when his mind was not working.

That was the last of his hallucinations. He was terribly embarrassed when we mentioned them to him later. They were not what he would do, he assured us.

He was right – they were *not* what he would do. That's what made them so disturbing.

Others have not been so fortunate.

Alan Whitmore's father's mind went long before his body. There's some question that he even knows he's in a care facility. "He's quite happy in his own little world," Mary Whitmore commented sadly, when I asked about her husband.

Sometimes all that's left to motivate a caregiver is the memory of love.

Only one chance

With an aging parent in precarious health, you may have only one chance to get things right. If you make a mistake, an error in judgment, before you can do things differently or make amends, your parent's health may already have changed. Then you're faced, once again, with a totally new and unfamiliar situation.

Almost by accident – it certainly wasn't by planning – I think I did some things right. If I were to summarize my insights, it would probably be this: *avoid extremes.* Don't impose any more changes than necessary on your parent. Grant them the dignity of making as many decisions as possible on their own, of retaining as much control as possible over their own lives. At the same time, don't do too little. Don't abandon them. A hands-off attitude now could lead to more serious losses later.

Minimize the losses that they – and you – must experience. Now, and in the future.

David Bryson
He couldn't hold the thought

Most of the time, Dad was in good health. I used to visit Scotland fairly regularly, and I'd go out and play golf with him.

Actually, it was his golfing that finished him. He slipped on the golf course – he had a bit of a back problem anyway – and damaged his hip. They said he would never walk again. But he did.

Then a stroke disabled his left side. I was having some success in getting him to walk again, when he had another stroke. Now he couldn't walk, and he couldn't speak. Well, he could, but he couldn't complete his sentences. He'd search for the word that he needed, and he couldn't find it. He got so frustrated. One time, he couldn't get the last word out, and he stuttered and stammered, and finally, in sheer frustration, he blurted out, "Oh, Jesus Christ!" We both laughed at that. He still had his sense of humor.

After that second stroke, he had to move into a nursing home.

I thought his speech disability might be just muscular, that the words were still there inside but he couldn't express them. So I bought him a portable computer, figuring that if he couldn't say it, perhaps he could type it. But it wasn't a verbal block, it was a mind block. He just couldn't hold the thought long enough to express the sentence.

Elaine Towgood

The benefits of losing your mind

My mother has been gradually losing her mind for years.

At first, she didn't like the idea of moving here from Vancouver. But now she doesn't know where she is. It's been so much easier for us because she has no idea what's going on.

I got a telephone call from her the other night. She got to a telephone, somewhere in her residence.

"Elaine, are you coming to see me?" she asked.

"Where are you, Mum?"

"I don't know, but it's a very nice hotel."

"Are you sure it's a hotel, Mum? Look around. Are your own chairs and towels there?"

"I don't know. I think it's a hotel. Yes, I'm sure it's a hotel. Can you come soon? I don't know how long I can stay here."

"I can't come today, Mum. But I can come the day after tomorrow."

"What day is that?"

"That's Monday, Mum."

"Will I be here that long?"

I could hear her talking to someone else in the background: "Will I still be here on Monday?"

I assured her: "Yes, Mum, I think you'll still be there."

It wouldn't matter if I went in once a week, or every day, or every other month, she really wouldn't know the difference. Her short-term memory is gone – all she can remember of me is from years and years ago.

❧

SIX

—

Becoming an Advocate

As aging parents grow more frail, they no longer have the energy to fight their own battles. They need someone to stand up for them.

People whose minds are slipping a little, who are sick, or just plain tired, often need an advocate. They need someone who will go to bat for them when they barely have the energy to get up to the plate, let alone score a home run.

But even if your parent is relatively healthy and energetic, they may still need you, on occassion, to stand by, ready to step in if someone tries to take advantage of them. A friend of mine recently accompanied her mother who was shopping for some new appliances. Her mother, who is still living on her own, discussed the pros and cons of the various models and negotiated a price with the salesman. In this situation, my friend was simply there as "insurance," to make sure her mother got a fair deal and was treated well. My own advocacy didn't come into focus until my father's health collapsed and he had to move into an institution.

My father had been released from one of his many trips to the hospital. He was back in the intermediate care facility. He actually seemed to be improving a little bit. He hadn't had to be rushed back to hospital for almost two weeks.

He moved very slowly around his room. I expected that. He didn't have much strength to work with. But I noticed that he lowered himself extremely gently into his easy chair. His face didn't carry much expression during those days, but what expression there was conveyed increased pain as he tried to sit down.

"Are you okay?" I asked. It was a silly question. Of course he wasn't okay. He was near dying. But fortunately, he was past pointing that out to me.

"Hemorrhoids," he grunted, once he had gotten himself settled.

"Have you told the nurses?" I persisted.

He nodded.

"They can treat these things, you know."

"I know," he said. He paused while he caught his breath again. "They don't… (pause again for breath)… listen to me."

I didn't understand that. This was my father, after all – the person whose knowledge and insight I had trusted since I had been a small child. It simply had not crossed my mind that others might not listen to him. That they might not pay much attention to what he said. It had not occurred to me that he might need someone to speak on his behalf. It certainly had not occurred to me that I could be a more credible advocate for him than he could be for himself.

A voice for the voiceless

In fact, anyone who is old, and sick, and tired, needs an advocate.

At that time, I was still fairly low on the learning curve. I should have gone and told the nurses myself about his hemorrhoids. They would probably have listened to me and done something.

In fairness to the nursing staff, they probably heard about a lot of imagined ailments from other residents who had long since lost touch with reality. They had not yet made a distinction between those patients and Dad, who was still very much in his right mind, even if he was physically weaker than many others. So when he complained about a bad case of hemorrhoids, they ignored him. They assumed that he was disoriented.

But as an outsider – and, as well, the outsider who paid the bills – they might have believed me.

Alternatively, I could have called his family doctor. I didn't. I still expected my father to look after himself. So I simply increased his stress levels by insisting that he get the nurses to do something about his discomfort. As a result, he suffered for the rest of the week, until the doctor came around on his regular visit to Crofton Manor. Only then were Dad's hemorrhoids recognized and treated.

Despite that slip-up, once their mistake was pointed out to them, Crofton's nursing staff never made it again. From that time on, if Dad drew their attention to upset digestion, dizziness, or any other problem, they responded promptly. A three-week bout of diarrhea was painfully obvious from his laundry basket. A vicious attack of gout, brought on by declining kidney function, was not as apparent. It hit his feet and his wrists. He couldn't stand, couldn't hold a pencil, couldn't even operate the remote control for his television set. But as soon as he told the duty nurse, she called his doctor, who adjusted Dad's medications immediately.

Institutions look after themselves first

Not all nursing homes are that cooperative – and very few hospitals are. They have an institution to run. They have schedules to keep, and tasks to fulfill. Sometimes "getting the job done" encourages callousness toward helpless people. The television program *Sixty Minutes* broadcast one episode in which a hidden camera caught nursing home aides slam-dunking patients out of their wheelchairs into their beds. Without the camera, they'd probably have gotten away with it.

If a patient complained, and you were in administration, who would you be more likely to believe? A bewildered, confused, and perhaps hallucinating old person? Or an apparently lucid, articulate, member of your own staff?

You may be tempted to make the same judgment if your parent tells you about being poorly treated. After all, you've just moved your parent into an institution because, you've become convinced, your parent is no longer capable of looking after himself or herself anymore. He forgets things; she imagines things.

Don't leap to conclusions. If your parent complains of maltreatment, listen. Don't dismiss the story as an old person's imagination inventing problems to gain attention or to seek sympathy. How consistent is the story? Is there any corroborating evidence? You may be the only person who cares enough to right a dangerous situation.

That kind of abuse is more likely to happen in smaller, privately run care institutions than in large public hospitals. Private homes and care facilities tend to have fewer inspections, and fewer people around to witness abuse. And when a small group of people work closely together, peer pressure can inhibit whistle-blowers.

Hospitals vary in the quality of care they give their patients. The meals served to my father in the hospital on the University of British Columbia campus were exponentially more appetizing than the meals Joan's aunt received in a small inland hospital, for example. But when I compare both hospitals with what I remember from earlier visits, I believe hospitals in general treat patients better than they used to. Visiting hours are more flexible. Meals are served with an insulating cover to keep them warmer, and patients have a few more menu choices offered to them.

But the meals still come around on the hospital's schedule, whether the patient is ready for them or not. Often, Dad was dozing when his dinner arrived. The aide delivered the tray to Dad's bed table, and left it there. Even with an insulating cover, by the time Dad woke up, his soup was often cold, his mashed potatoes as appetizing as congealing concrete. Little wonder he often sent the tray back untouched.

One estimate I read suggested that 50 percent of elderly hospitalized patients suffer malnutrition. I would have guessed an even higher proportion – based not so much on the quality of the meals, but on the ability and willingness of the patients to make the effort to eat.

Lack of adequate nutrition will handicap your parent's ability to re-gain enough strength to get out of hospital. But you can do something to help. Down the hall, not far from the nursing station, Sharon found a little room not much bigger than a closet, with a microwave oven and a refrig-erator. The sign called it a "Nutrition Room." We took Dad's soup, pota-toes, or coffee, down the hall and reheated them in the microwave oven. Other times, we got him a cup of chilled apple juice from the refrigerator.

Theoretically, that room was out of bounds to us. It had a sign on the door: "Staff Only." We ignored it. So should you, in a similar situa-tion. The institution is there to serve its patients; the patients and visi-tors are not there to serve the institution.

Make friends with the staff

I'm not suggesting you should simply disregard rules. That would alien-ate the nursing staff, who are your most valuable allies in any kind of institution. Rather, get them on your side.

No care facility, these days, has a surplus of staff. Nurses are always under pressure to get more done, in less time, with fewer people. Our use of the "Nutrition Room" may not have been strictly within official rules. But it saved the nurses from responding to yet another room call.

You can do other things. Remember to say "Please" and "Thank you," for example. Too often, nurses get taken for granted. A bit of ap-preciation helps. When you treat them with respect, they're more likely to treat you and your parent the same way.

One book I read suggested bringing flowers for the nursing station occasionally.

Get to know your parent's nurses by name. "Excuse me, Carol…" wins a lot more attention than "Hey, you…" Without forcing them to take time away from their other duties, try to engage your parent's nurses briefly in conversation while they're with your parent, so that you get to know each other as individuals, not just as functions. Carol is more than just a body in a uniform who straightens your parent's bed periodically, just as you are more than a body who sits by the bed and weeps.

In the same way, help the nurses to recognize your parent as more than an illness. Bring in a picture of your parent in his or her better days, to put on the nightstand by the bed. Perhaps a picture of your mother bouncing a grandchild in her lap. Of your father, water-skiing. It's all too easy for nursing staff to define patients by their illness. So your father becomes "the pneumonia in 403C," your mother "the kidney in 213A." Anything that helps the medical staff see your parent as something more than a grab bag of symptoms will result in more humane care.

Does the hospital still clothe its patients in those embarrassing gowns that won't stay closed? A second gown will keep your parent's shoulders warmer, and reduce the humiliation of exposing a bare behind to the rest of the ward when moving around. Bringing a housecoat from home is another alternative. Ask if the hospital will let patients wear their own familiar pajamas.

Establishing some sort of personal context becomes particularly important if your parent suffers from depression, or gets disoriented, or tends to be snappish anyway – and who wouldn't, given the losses and disruptions most elderly people go through? It's always harder for medical staff to respond sensitively and compassionately to someone who is rude or uncommunicative.

Keeping the records straight

It took me some time to absorb the notion that my father, who had watched out for me for so long, now needed an advocate to watch out for his interests. (Though my examples are mostly health related, remember that advocacy can also involve your parent's dealings with all kinds of government agencies, insurance companies, banks, stores, auto mechanics, home repair firms – all those daily relationships that, when you're younger, you take for granted.)

Dad's transfers into hospital often coincided, by some chance, with trips that I had planned to make to visit him anyway. One time, after Crofton had called an ambulance for him, Grace, his favorite nurse, told Dad she would call me. "Will Jim be at home?" she asked.

Dad checked his watch. "He's probably already somewhere on the road between Merritt and Hope," he guessed.

I was. And so I reached the hospital while Dad was still in the emergency room, waiting to be admitted. The emergency staff let me come in and sit with Dad as soon as they had completed blood tests, an electrocardiogram, etc.

He looked terribly old and frail, propped up in a far corner of the room. His skin was almost as gray as his hair. He had a drooping eyelid at the best of times – now it hung so slack he could barely see out of that eye.

"Hi, Dad," I said, lamely.

"Oh, son," he said, looking miserable. "I didn't want to bother you..."

He got terribly fed up with the hospital's admission procedures. "They ask me the same questions every time," he muttered. "I tell them that they should just pull my file and look up their records from the last time."

"So why don't they?" I asked.

"Regulations. They say they have to ask, each time."

They would have obtained more accurate information from the old records than from Dad's answers. He was too debilitated to answer intelligently. Fortunately, I was there when a nurse came around with a clipboard to ask all those routine admission questions.

"Do you have any allergies?" she asked.

"None," he replied.

I had to remind him of his allergies to narcotics. Especially to codeine, which induced pancreatitis – "excruciatingly painful," his doctor had told me.

"Oh, yes," he said, vaguely.

He also forgot to mention that he had a pacemaker, though they would certainly have discovered that sooner or later. And when the nurse asked for his address, he gave his former apartment address, rather than Crofton Manor.

Medication problems

Advocacy may mean venturing into areas in which you have no expertise. Like pharmaceutical medications, for example.

If you're looking after an aging parent in your own home, you'll have to learn what pills your mother or father has to take, and when. You may have to count out the pills, and keep full containers locked away so that your parent cannot accidentally overdose. If elderly parents have dementia, they may take their pills too often, or not often enough. In addition, some elderly folks don't like taking pills. They don't even want to take painkillers such as Aspirin, because they have learned, sometime or other, that depending on pills is a sign of weakness. Or it could become addictive. Or something. So they take their pills under protest, and may even tuck them into a cheek to spit out later.

That, fortunately, was one area where I did not have to worry much. In Crofton Manor, the nursing staff handled *all* the medications – other than over-the-counter vitamins, cold and headache pills, and digestive antacids. They counted out the dosage at every meal, delivered it to the table, and watched to make sure the residents took their medication properly.

Nor did I have to concern myself much about the kinds of pills Dad had to take. My father's physician, Dr. Stephen Roberts, had been a pharmacist before switching to medicine. So he kept a very close eye on Dad's medications.

Others have not been so fortunate. Dr. William Molloy, in his book *What Are We Going to Do Now?* cites example after example of elderly patients whose main problem is either too many medications, or conflicting medications. Molloy implies that many physicians get impatient with the elderly. Rather than take the time to find out what's really going on – including psychological and emotional causes – they simply prescribe another pill. If the patient is simultaneously seeing a variety of specialists, the accumulation of prescriptions can have unexpected effects. To compound the problem, many of these elders are accustomed to treating doctors as authority figures. They would not dream of challenging a doctor's diagnosis.

Molloy suggests that a key function for caregiving children is to act as liaison – to make sure each doctor or specialist knows what the others have prescribed, to ask questions, to lobby for overall reductions in medication.

The information you need

You don't have to be an expert on pharmaceuticals to ask intelligent questions. Because your expertise lies in a different area – you're an expert on your parent. No professional has known your parent as long as you have; no professional cares as much about your parent as you do. So you have a perfect right to ask questions about matters that affect your parent.

Here are some questions you could ask, if you haven't been given adequate answers already:

1. About the medication itself
- What is it supposed to do?
- How will we know if it's working?
- What is it contraindicated for? (That's jargon for "What conditions will it make worse?")
- How does it interact with other medications your parent is already taking?
- Do we need the brand-name version, or would a generic version work as well?
- Can we accomplish the same result by other methods? (For example, alternative treatments such as acupuncture, meditation, herbal remedies, diet, or exercise.)

2. About the usage of the medication

- How many, how often? With or without food or drink?
- For how long? Even after the symptoms have ended?
- What happens if he/she forgets?
- Would a lower dosage work? (Dosages may vary according to the person's weight, age, gender, etc.)
- Are there any foods, drinks, or activities to avoid while taking it?

3. About the effects of the medication

- Could it become addictive?
- Are there any long-term effects? (In case your parent has to take it for the rest of his/her life.)
- How will we know if it's causing problems? (Allergies, adverse reactions.)

If you need more information, there are several ways of finding it. Look first at the most obvious, and perhaps most overlooked, source – the package the medication comes in. Most decongestants, for example, warn that they should not be taken by anyone with glaucoma or prostate problems. Ask questions of the various doctors and specialists. Or talk to your local pharmacist. A pharmacist will probably not risk contradicting a doctor directly, but you may get some good leads to follow up. If you still don't get the answers you need, try reference libraries. (Or search the Internet.) Vast volumes exist that list every conceivable prescription drug, along with its side effects. But don't be frightened off by the sheer volume of information. You don't need to know *all* that stuff. You only need to know about the limited number of medications prescribed for your parent, and how they might interact.

Exploit your ignorance

You may find it hard to question a professional's wisdom. It goes against the grain to admit ignorance – and worse, to use that ignorance to challenge someone with superior knowledge. But for your parent's sake, you may have to do it.

Most older people will not make a fuss about themselves. Part of their ethos, their upbringing, was not to draw attention to themselves. They were brought up on maxims like, "Children should be seen and not heard," and "Silence is golden." Lessons learned in childhood persist through life. Indeed, they may grow stronger as elderly people grow more frail. Just as memories of childhood may be more clear than those of last week, so a child's deference to adults may displace a lifetime of sturdy self-reliance.

As parents become more frail, too, they have less energy available to fight their own battles.

That was a hard lesson for me to learn. During the months after my father was first hospitalized with his two silent heart attacks, when he was so weakened that his own doctor didn't think he would ever get out of hospital again, I thought I was there to give him love and support, not to demand better treatment. I was happy to crank his bed up and down, to find a position that eased his chest congestion. I gladly smoothed out the bedclothes when they got bunched up beneath his bony behind. I willingly brought him apple juice or ginger ale. I helped him out of bed into the commode chair, and wheeled him to the bathroom – and when he was too weak to use the bathroom, I cheerfully helped him with the urinal or the bedpan.

But at first it didn't occur to me to raise questions with the nursing staff – much less with the resident physicians – to find out what was happening to him.

Sharon made a much better advocate than I did. She had studied enough physiology at university that she wouldn't be overwhelmed by medical mumbo jumbo. She buttonholed the medical team on their morning rounds. She wanted to know exactly what medications they had prescribed for her grandfather, and why. She expected a full explanation from the intern about the coronary function tests Dad had taken. And when the meal delivered to his bed wasn't what he and his doctor had ordered, she marched the tray right back to the nursing station, and got it changed.

I learned a lot from her. Occasionally, I got enough nerve to put it into practice.

Dad was in a teaching hospital. Every morning, the supervising internist paraded through the wards at the head of a column of students, like the Pied Piper leading rats through Hamelin. He checked patients' charts that were hanging at the foot of the bed. He talked about the patients as if they weren't there, and swept majestically on. One morning, I caused some commotion by interrupting his flow of wisdom. I asked him a question, thus inviting him to talk to me, too. The students looked shocked.

I'm not sure what reaction I expected from him. Imperious outrage, perhaps. A put-down or a brush-off, more likely. To my surprise, he seemed to welcome my interest and concern, and explained things quickly and simply.

Heartened by that encounter, I began to make it a customary practice to ask questions. Of Dad's own doctor. Of the residents as they came around. Of the nurses. I didn't always get satisfactory answers. But I never got a brush-off or put-down from anyone. Most actually seemed pleased that someone cared enough to ask.

I attribute some of my success to asking questions, rather than launching missiles of criticism or complaint. Questions can draw previously unnoticed concerns to the other person's attention. Questions can express concern. They also imply an open mind. Complaints and criticisms, on the other hand, usually denote a mind that's already closed, a mind already made up about what's wrong and whose fault it is.

Questions worth asking

Inevitably, your parent will undergo tests. Sometimes those tests will lead to treatments, sometimes to surgery. The questions you might ask – indeed, *should* ask – include some of the following:

1. The purpose of this procedure

- What's it supposed to do or show?
- What will happen if we don't do it?
- What are the risks of doing it, and the risks of not doing it?

2. Alternatives to this procedure

- How else could we accomplish the same goal? (For example, could nutrition or diet or exercises accomplish the same thing as medication or even surgery?)
- Are there other kinds of treatments that would work? (For example, acupuncture, chiropractic, meditation, therapeutic touch.)

3. The prognosis

- How much pain/discomfort will be involved?
- What's the recovery time?
- How much benefit does it really provide? (If surgery is inevitable anyway, why inflict this test? If the procedure won't result in either recovery or significantly extended life, why bother?)
- What symptoms do I need to watch out for afterwards?

4. Administration

- If a test, will the results be available to other professionals or departments (to avoid repeating the procedure)?
- Where will I find my parent during the recovery period?
- How much will this cost? (Even if your parent is covered by medicare or insurance, why incur unnecessary or extravagant expenses?)

One bit of advice that almost every book recommended – take notes. Carry a notebook with you. When you ask questions, jot down the answers you get.

That's particularly important any time a doctor gives instructions about treatment. If you can't go with your parent to a medical appointment, find someone else who can go along. As older people's minds move more slowly, even those without memory loss tend to focus on only a few instructions, and miss the rest.

"We had to stop letting her go to the doctor alone," one woman said of her mother. "She didn't know what they had done, and she couldn't tell us. She didn't know if there were medications that they had prescribed, or anything she should be doing or not doing."

When a diagnosis comes as a shock, even *you* may have trouble remembering instructions. The doctor keeps talking, but your mind locks on to "cancer" or "Alzheimer's" and hears nothing more. Making notes serves two valuable purposes: it helps to keep your mind functioning, and it gives you some mental anchor points on which to reconstruct the conversation later. At the very least, it gives you an excuse to call back: "I can't read my scribbled notes – what did you say about…?"

Similarly, whenever your parent checks out of hospital, make sure you have a *written* list of instructions for treatment, medication, and therapy. Hospitals *should* provide this automatically, but they don't always. If you don't get it, ask for it. You, or the care facility your parent moves into, will need it.

Beating your head against bureaucracy

But remember that it is not only medical matters that call for an advocate. My father's period of almost total disability coincided with income tax time. Even in his weakened state, he could still recognize that the deadline for filing papers was approaching. It bothered him that he could do nothing about it.

So that became my job.

Finding and gathering the existing receipts was relatively easy, once he told me where to look for them. But some of the necessary papers were missing.

Dad's neat hand-lettered lists indicated some sizable charitable donations he had made, for which we could not find any receipts. In his state of mind and health, Dad could not have called those charities to get duplicate receipts from them. We telephoned, wrote, cajoled, and pleaded. Mostly, we succeeded.

The hardest duplicates to get were the missing statements of income. Canadian banks, insurance companies, and pension funds issue T3, T4, and T5 forms, which have to be attached to tax returns. Some of those were missing too. After going through every nook and cranny in Dad's apartment, I spent hours writing letters and making telephone calls, to persuade these organizations that a) I had a right to make this contact; b) they should check their records; and c) they should issue a duplicate.

Getting an interest income statement from Canada Savings Bonds proved the most difficult problem. The person I reached, at the far end of the country, did her best to help. But her regulations prevented her from releasing any information unless I could first give her the information that *she* needed to confirm my right to act on my father's behalf. And no address that I gave her matched the address on her computer. Finally, after much fencing around, it dawned on me – Dad had bought those bonds through his investment broker. Her records showed not his address but the broker's!

If you don't do that kind of sleuthing for your parent, who will? You can't expect an accountant to do it – or if you do, it will cost you big bucks.

Other venues

As you will discover, there is an almost limitless range of situations where your parent may need the help of a calm, objective, but firm advocate. Here are but a few.

- *Family conflicts.* When various factions in a larger family disagree about treatment, or about handling finances, the parent can get sucked into a vortex that saps energy he or she needs just to survive. If you can't resolve the dispute yourself, bring in mediation.
- *Home care.* Not all home care workers are created equal. Some will do all that's asked of them, and more. Others will do a half-hour's shopping and spend the rest of their allotted time drinking coffee and gos-

siping. Your parent may not feel like protesting – either out of charity or fear of reprisals. You may have to contact the local supervisor.

- *Housekeeping and maintenance.* Home care workers are only allowed to do certain things, such as shopping, vacuuming, and some meal preparation. Their duties rarely include windows. Hired housekeepers also tend not to do windows. (They may also shirk dusting bookshelves and other areas that an elderly person may not notice.) To reduce allergies and improve visibility, you may have to contract specialized services periodically, to clean windows and carpets, for example.

- *Living conditions.* Make sure your parent has adequate light. Older people need nearly three times as much light as younger people. In the hospital, ask for a bed near a window. In a care facility or at home, increase the power of light bulbs, and position lamps so that the light falls properly on the book, magazine, or needlework. Clear a path to the bathroom, so that your parent won't stumble over something at night. Install night lights in hallways and bathrooms.

Making house calls

One other small example – although to a frail and debilitated person, it may not seem small. My father was due for a dental checkup, shortly after he had his heart attacks. He didn't make it, of course. While he was near death, the state of his teeth mattered no more to him than the price of green cheese. But as his health began to improve slightly, he started fussing about his teeth. His nurses at Crofton Manor could offer him little help. Most of the other residents were past caring about their teeth; the few who were strong enough called a taxi to take them to their dental appointments.

If anything was going to happen, I would have to make it happen. I called his dentist to explain the situation. "We thought something must have happened," the receptionist sympathized. "He's usually so good about being on time for things."

"He's in a nursing home," I said. "There's no way that he's going to be able to come to your office. Even if I drove him there, he hasn't the stamina to cope with a regular appointment."

The receptionist checked her records. Dad's appointment was for a cleaning, not for fillings or major dental work.

"Is there such a thing in the city as a traveling hygienist?" I asked. "Someone who could go to him and do the job there?"

"You're in luck," she replied. "We do have a dental hygienist who makes house calls."

A week later, Dad had his teeth cleaned. In the Manor's hairdressing salon. He felt much better.

The manor was so impressed that they invited the hygienist to make regular visits, to serve other patients who were similarly unable to get out to their regular dentists.

I think of it as a small victory for advocacy.

Janice Leonard

He can't talk, but he can respond

I feel a lot closer to my father now than I ever did before. And he's closer to me. He knows that someone loves him. You become closer when you become a caretaker for someone. But it's hard on family dynamics. It changes your relationships with the other members of your family. I find it better to see him by myself, rather than with them. We spend a lot of time touching and stroking. He can still respond to that.

You have to spend time – a lot of time – with someone in Dad's condition to understand that he is still capable of communicating.

I was not in favor of committing him to a care home. It's not really care. It's convenience, for the staff. They have him tied into a chair. I wanted him to get physiotherapy. Before he went in, I was getting him able to do some walking, some activities. Now he's just tied down. He was walking twice a day down to the mailbox. He'd walk the dog. There is no quality of life for him in the home.

He's not really capable of making decisions. But he can participate in them. At a meeting, with the Director of Nursing, I wanted Dad to be present. He can't talk, but he can react. He can respond.

It's very difficult when you take away someone's independence.

Anonymous*

Just putting in time between paychecks

Nursing homes are not always the answer that they seem to be. My dad was in one for rehab after a stroke and it was awful. Yes, he had a bed and there were meals; the beds were made and people were supposedly assigned to him. But they forgot to give him his medicine at times. They had to be told to bathe him. And if he didn't go to meals, then he didn't get fed – and no one even thought to take them to him.

I found that the employees were uncaring and basically just putting in time between paychecks and I wouldn't wish it on my least favorite person on earth!

Needless to say, I became my Dad's patient advocate. Somehow we got through it. Since our experience, I have spoken to many of us "sandwich" middle-agers and I find that what we experienced is typical.

What we did find worthwhile, though, was "adult day-care" facilities. They not only give the caregivers a break, but the cared-for actually do get cared for! Combined with at-home health aide use, the ending of life has quality to it. And it is less costly too.

There was a point at the end of my Dad's life where we were going to put him back into a nursing home – his kidneys were shutting down and he needed constant care and was bedridden. But we knew if we had to resort to that, we as a family would be a part of his daily care, to ensure that he would in fact get care. As it turned out, we were spared that when he passed away.

*From the Internet, *Third Age* page, no name given.

SEVEN

The Will, The Way

There's nothing like facing death to raise one's awareness of tasks still not done. For far too many people, of any age, one of those not-done tasks is writing a will.

It's amazing how many people put off writing their wills until it's too late. A 1993 survey for the Trust Companies Association of Canada (quoted in *You Can't Take It with You*, by Sandra E. Foster, Toronto: John Wiley, 1998) found "that only half of Canadians over 18 have a will." Similar figures apply for the United States.

Or, put another way, roughly half of our parents die without leaving any directions for the distribution of their estates. Whatever they leave will be divided up according to the laws of the province or state they live in, regardless of their wishes. The black-sheep daughter who hasn't shown up for 30 years will get exactly the same as the son who looked after his senile mother in his own home for her final decade of life.

Get a will written

So the first thing you can do for an aging parent – and for yourself – is to make sure that he or she has a will. If your parent already has a will, make sure it has been updated.

And make sure it is legally valid. Handwritten wills may or may not be considered legally acceptable in your province or state. But acceptability aside, a handwritten will can raise all kinds of legal problems because of ambiguous wording. Unless the will says, with no qualifications of any kind, "I leave everything to _____," you should get some form of qualified legal assistance. At the very least, get some standard will forms, available in many stationery stores, where you or your parent only have to fill in the blanks.

But be careful. In Canadian law, generic forms are *usually* acceptable, provided they're filled out correctly. But not always. Canadian Probate Offices have reported that some forms *do* cause difficulties. Caution is even more necessary in the United States. Canada has only 13 different jurisdictions with varying rules and regulations; the U.S. has 50, coupled with an even more independent tradition. Some will accept handwritten wills, some won't. Some will accept generic documents; some will throw them out on the smallest technicalities. Before using any generic document, or writing an original, always check with the relevant government office to find out what they will accept as a will.

I don't want to go into detail about how to write a will. First, I'm not a lawyer, so my advice has no legal force. Second, every province and state has its own rules and regulations, which vary just enough that advice based on British Columbia law could cause complications in Quebec or Indiana. And third, it's worth getting expert advice. A will is certainly going to penalize someone if doesn't take into account the different kinds of benefits that result from a) insurance policies payable to a beneficiary; b) the sale of a principal home; c) cashing in RRSPs, 401(k)s, IRAs, or SEPs; d) death benefits from pension plans; e) and capital gains on investments.

A will put together without expert advice may appear to divide an estate equally among surviving children, but end up giving one or more of the children a tax-free windfall, and leave another child responsible for paying off a crippling final income-tax bill. Suppose, for example, that the estate goes to three children. One gets the family home. The other two get equivalent dollar value: one in life insurance, the last from a registered retirement savings plan – which, in Canada, accumulates value tax-free until it's cashed in. The family home and the insurance will transfer full value to their beneficiaries without penalty; the registered savings plan will probably be taxed at around 50 percent.

…and know where it is

You don't really need to know what's in your parent's will. It doesn't come into effect until after the parent's death. In that sense, it can't affect your present life. Or at least, it shouldn't. If it *does* affect your present life, there's probably something wrong going on. Either you're basing your behavior on what you expect to inherit, or your parent is using the provisions of the will – like wielding a club – to influence you.

From a moral and ethical perspective, it may be better *not* to know what's in that will. In this rare instance, ignorance may indeed be bliss. Because if you're a favored beneficiary, you could later be accused by other relatives of only doing whatever you did for the bequest you expected to get eventually. And if you discover that you're not going to get very much, you might be tempted to abandon your parent just when he or she most needs you.

Love and caring are not things you can measure in terms of monetary worth. If you give care only because of the benefit you expect to reap, it's not love. It's not compassion. It's not even pity. It's greed. The way you treat your aging parent should reflect the kind of person you are, and the kind of relationship you have with your parent. Better you should feel good about yourself, when it's all over, than merely feel you were appropriately compensated.

But although you don't need to know what's in the will, you definitely need to know where the will is. Because when your parent dies, the executor will need to have access to that will. "It's in the bank box" is not good enough. As soon as the bank learns of your parent's death, it will seal the bank box. To get access to it, you will have to prove that you are the executor and are legally entitled to examine and list its contents. You can't do that easily if the proof you need – the will – is locked inside the box.

So there should be at least two notarized copies of the will, preferably three. The first belongs with your parent, and will probably be kept in the bank box. Another copy – often the original – should be on file with your parent's lawyer. A third copy, if there is one, should go directly to the executor. If you're that executor, to avoid even a suspicion of having been influenced by the will's contents, you can keep the will inside a sealed, unopened, envelope.

Notice that I specified "notarized" copies. A simple photocopy isn't worth the paper it's copied on. Banks, insurance companies, and government agencies will usually require notarized copies, that is, copies bearing the seal and signature of someone, as one of my dictionaries puts it, "legally empowered to witness and certify the validity of documents." A notarized copy is just as valid as an original.

As an aside, though, you don't necessarily need a lawyer or a notary public to provide "notarized copies." In my province, a host of others can certify a document. Constance Mungall's *Probate Guide for British Columbia* (Self-Counsel Press, 17th edition, 1998) lists 19 qualified positions, from a bank manager to a medical doctor, a minister to a postmaster. Basically, if a person can certify a passport photo, they can certify a document.

But you may find it hard to convince a bank of that.

Get a lawyer to help

Legal and accounting advice costs money. It's worth it.

Unfortunately, writing a will often doesn't seem urgent – until it becomes desperately urgent.

My father, for example, had had a will as long as I can remember. He was a very responsible person. But he replaced his will when my mother died, and again when he retired, when he remarried, when his second wife died…

After those two heart attacks disabled him, he became acutely aware of his own mortality. During the previous year, he had been doing some preparatory work with his lawyer to revise his will. He had taken his time about changing it. Suddenly, that revised will became urgent, a priority.

"He's really worried about his will," Sharon told me, when I came down from the Okanagan Valley to help her move Dad into his new quarters at Crofton Manor.

"You'll find a draft of the will in the desk drawer," he told me, after giving me a frail hug.

When his health deteriorated, and he was sent back to hospital, his first instruction was, "You'll have to get in touch with the lawyer about the will."

"Did you find the will? Did you get in touch with the lawyer?" he asked the next time I visited him.

In fact, if he had died without changing his will, it would not have made much difference. Aside from specific bequests to Joan and Sharon, he left everything to me, as his only child. I was also his executor and trustee. His will included other provisions, fairly standard, for distributing his estate if I died before him, and if the others in line to inherit also died or were otherwise unable to receive his assets.

But suddenly the revisions to that will became a matter of desperate urgency for him. He wanted things in order before he died.

I shuttled several drafts of his new will to him in the hospital. Each time, his lawyer had helpfully underlined the changes in red.

Some of the red-underlined changes weren't quite what Dad had intended. He was in a four-bed ward at the time, without an accessible telephone. At Dad's insistence, we loaded him into a wheelchair, and wheeled him down the corridor to the pay phone near the nursing station, so that he could talk to his lawyer directly.

Eventually, all the details were correct.

House calls

Then came the problem of getting the new will signed and witnessed. Dad could sign it with no problem, although his handwriting was much shakier and less confident than it had been a few months before. And although he was weak and tired, he was still "of sound mind."

But a will requires witnesses. Objective witnesses, who have no personal interest in the will's contents. As a beneficiary, I couldn't witness it. Neither could Joan and Sharon, the other two most available people.

You might think a couple of nurses could witness a will. That's what I thought. I was wrong. Their training cautions them against getting involved in what can sometimes turn into a protracted legal battle – especially if a very sick person unpredictably makes a major change in beneficiaries. Angry family members could claim the patient was not in his or her right mind at the time, not mentally competent to make those changes. The nurses become the punching bag for everyone's frustrations.

We could have called on friends and colleagues to come to the hospital. But at the time, we were all so overwhelmed with our new responsibilities, that possibility didn't occur to us. We felt like strangers in an alien land.

I explained all this to Dad's lawyer, Alfred Field.

"That's no problem," he said. "I can come out to the hospital."

A lawyer who makes house calls? Indeed, it was true – although he did qualify his offer with "only in special cases." And he brought his secretary along as the second witness.

When I arrived at the hospital ward the next morning, I found the curtains drawn around Dad's bed. I thought perhaps the nurse might be performing some kind of routine treatment – changing his intravenous drip, giving him a shave, changing his hospital gown… I sat down on a chair by the door to wait.

Curtains around a hospital bed conceal the person from sight, but they don't restrict sound at all. I heard Dad cough within the closed curtains. A woman's voice said, "There that does it." Then, to my surprise, I heard a rumbling male voice: "That's fine, Dr. Taylor. That takes care of everything. Thank you."

And Dad's feeble voice creaked: "Thank *you* for coming."

The curtains zipped back, and Alfred Field came out with his secretary. The will was done. Dad could relax, at last.

Ripple effect

A word or two of confession, here. People tend to make their wills in times of crisis – and I'm no exception. Joan and I first made out our wills after our son Stephen was diagnosed with cystic fibrosis. CF is a hereditary genetic illness. At the time, it was considered terminal, and incurable – although a time-consuming regimen of treatment could prolong life. Lung transplants had not been attempted yet; the artificial enzymes that now enable CF patients to digest their food were still being developed. Stephen's health was precarious, and we were his only lifeline. As the extent of his illness, and his need for consistent therapy, became more evident to us, we had to worry about what would happen to him, if anything happened to the two of us. We needed someone we could count on to take over his care.

This was not a task we could expect anyone to undertake lightly. In those early days, clinics were still learning about treatment. Dr. Douglas Crozier, the pioneer of CF treatment in Canada, told us that they didn't really know if some of the treatments they prescribed were helping. "But," he asked pointedly, "would you rather have your son have the treatments, even if they're unnecessary, or kick yourself for the rest of your life because he didn't have something that might have made a difference?" So, at that time, we gave him 2 – 3 hours of physiotherapy every day, pounding his chest to joggle mucus out of his lungs. We fed him a special high-fat diet, to help his blood carry more oxygen. He gulped handfuls of pills to help him digest every meal, every snack. Without the medical plan I had through my employment, the pills alone would have wiped out more than 25 percent of my gross income. Stephen slept at night in a mist tent, inhaling a fine vapor intended to dilute the mucus clogging his bronchial tubes. That meant Joan had to strip his bed every day, wash his sheets, his blankets, his teddy bear, and put them through the dryer.

Not many would willingly undertake such onerous responsibilities. Fortunately for us, a couple who had been friends since university days were willing. So we drafted our first wills, naming them executors and guardians. Most of our financial provisions were set up to ensure they were not penalized for their generosity.

Stephen's eventual death was another crisis. It prompted us to revise our wills. Our friends' commitment was no longer necessary. By then, too, Sharon was considered an adult, and no longer needed a guardian or trustee to control her inheritance.

By the time of my father's illness, we had not had a family crisis for almost 15 years. There hadn't been any pressing need to amend our wills in all that time – although our assets had changed significantly. Both our wills were out of date.

When we came back from Vancouver, we started the process of revising our own wills. This time, *before* it became a matter of desperate urgency.

Give it away now

A will is, in a sense, an attempt to achieve immortality. It has no value at all during our lifetimes. It comes into effect only after we die. By writing a will, we try to control our assets after death. By doing our wills, Joan and I define what will happen to our possessions – house, car, china, silver, books and tools, savings and investments – when we're no longer there to deal with them ourselves.

But there's no reason why we have to wait until death to dispose of our assets. We can, if we choose to, put our wishes into action right now. That is, we can give our assets away, just as they would be distributed by an executor after our deaths.

A neighbor's father did that. He had been a farmer in Alberta all his life. When he realized his health would not let him continue farming, he gave the farm to his children. They were going to get it anyway, he reasoned. So why keep them hanging until he died? He kept just enough to support himself, and literally gave away the farm.

My father had a collection of oil paintings. Back in his university days, he wondered about becoming an artist rather than a minister. Back then, Canada's "Group of Seven" was just beginning to build a reputation for its uniquely Canadian vision of landscapes. The members of the Group spent a lot of time sketching in northern Ontario. When they came back to Toronto, to expand their oil sketches into finished paintings, they made their headquarters in Lawren Harris's Rosedale studio, only a few blocks from the University of Toronto, where my father was studying. He made friends with some of the members of the Group, and with other painters associated with them. He even took some lessons, briefly, from A. Y. Jackson.

Drawing on their inspiration and training, my father painted landscapes much of his life: in India, in Ireland, in Canada. Whenever he had a spare bit of money, he bought paintings. He couldn't afford the full-sized finished works by any of the established artists of the Group, or their students, associates, or mentors. But he could buy their oil sketches, usually done on 8" by 10" panels. Over the years, he collected several Manly MacDonalds, a couple each by H. S. Palmer and J. W. Beatty, an Eric Riordan... In his bank box, we found a personal note from A. Y. Jackson himself.

Long before his death, he started giving these paintings away. We've had some on our walls for almost 20 years.

After Sharon grew up and established her own home, he began giving other paintings to her. It's important, legally, that the gift actually be "delivered" into the new owner's hands. A signed label, stuck to the back of the picture, certified the date and the occasion when Dad handed the paintings over to his granddaughter.

Sharon's generosity, in turn, allowed him to continue to enjoy them. Although she now owned them, she was willing to loan them back to him while he lived. It turned out to be a valuable gesture.

Crofton Manor encouraged its residents to furnish their rooms with their own belongings, to make the space more personal. You never know what will personalize a space. For some, it's knickknacks, little souvenirs that bring back memories. For others, it will be a favorite chair, a quilt on the bed, a rug on the floor, a familiar desk or work space. For my father, it was those paintings.

For some people, familiar chairs, tables, and lamps ease the transition from living at home to living in an institution. But furniture had no value for my father. Most of the furniture in his apartment wasn't his, anyway. It had belonged to Chris, his second wife. He never changed it. In fact, he hardly bothered moving it. He adjusted the position of his own favorite chair, the one he sat in to watch soccer and curling on TV. But he simply walked around the chairs he didn't use, even if they were in his way.

So familiar furniture wouldn't make Dad's room feel like home. But the paintings did. He took four of his favorites from his apartment to his room at Crofton Manor. During the first two months after his initial heart attacks, when he was constantly in and out of hospital, he didn't have time – or energy – to hang any pictures. But when those pictures finally went up on his walls, we noticed a difference in his attitude. The paintings evoked memories for him, memories of when he was a younger man, when the world was just opening up before him, instead of gradually closing in. For the first time, he began to speak of Crofton as "home."

Reducing taxes

Reducing taxes should never be the primary reason for doing something – it lets tax regulations push your buttons, in effect – but it's always worth considering. If an asset, like my father's collection of paintings, is given away through a will, income tax authorities treat that transfer as a sale. The asset must be valued at the time of death, and if it has increased in value since it was purchased, the estate has to pay income tax on the capital gain.

But there are fewer restrictions on gifts freely given during a lifetime (although oil paintings, collections, and the like, *may* still be taxable). There are, in that sense, tax benefits in giving things away prior to death.

Another way to avoid paying unnecessary taxes after death may be to name a beneficiary. It's one reason why purchasing life insurance still has value, later in life. When the policy becomes payable – at death – the money goes directly to the beneficiary. It is not calculated into the value of the estate.

So increasing numbers of older people today are buying insurance policies which will cover their final income taxes. The policy can be taken out while both parents are still living. One parent's assets can pass directly to the spouse, without being taxed. But when the second parent dies, their combined assets will be taxed. Any stocks or mutual funds will be evaluated as of the date of death. The estate will have to pay tax on any gain in value – and since many parents have held these shares for decades, the capital gain can be startling. They've been increasing in value, often without ever being taxed, because they have never been sold. But when their owner dies, they are deemed to have been sold.

How much you will have to pay in income taxes, on your parent's behalf, depends on the size of the estate. If your parents managed to accumulate very little wealth, the final year of income will be taxed at the lowest rates. But if your parent had amassed considerable wealth – and a surprising number of elderly people don't spend the income they get from pensions and other sources – you may find the estate paying income taxes well above the 50 percent mark.

Naming a beneficiary *may* bypass that financial crunch. Because at the time of death, the beneficiary owns it. Not the estate.

That discovery drove Joan and me to check our investments. Most of them, we learned to our relief, name each other as beneficiary.

Dad had done much the same. Long ago. Unfortunately, he hadn't kept his beneficiaries up to date. When I started checking, I discovered that one of his annuities named Chris Fraser, his second wife, as beneficiary. She had been dead for 16 years. Before I could do anything with that policy, I had to provide the trust company with not just one but two death certificates: one for my father, to prove that he had died; one for Chris, to prove that she had predeceased him.

Not even one asset named me as beneficiary. But I only learned that *after* Dad had died.

I wish I had known earlier. The name of a beneficiary would have been easy to change while Dad was still alive. But I didn't know, and so we didn't do it.

Because like so many other families, we found it so difficult to talk about money.

John Congram

Firmly in control

My mother was still making all the decisions, up to a few weeks before she died from a massive stroke. My brother and I were co-executors, but we didn't have to exercise any authority until after she died. We resisted pressure from some relatives and friends who felt we should be making some of the decisions for our mother; they wondered if she was any longer capable of looking after herself.

It was her decision to move out of her house into an apartment, and then from the apartment into a room in a seniors home. We didn't have to deal with possessions, because she lined up everything she had. Then she invited in people who had been good to her, and gave each of them something. And it was thus out of our hands, and she had the benefit that she knew her things had gone to someone who would appreciate having something that had been hers.

❧

John Shearman

Advice for those who are younger

As one who has already passed the allotted biblical life span of three score and ten, I have a personal interest in death and dying.

I have three bits of advice for those who are younger and still of sound mind and body.

1. Make sure your will is up-to-date.
2. Write a power of attorney document for personal care stating as clearly as possible what you want to have done for you when you are no longer capable of making such decisions for yourself.
3. Make known to your heirs what you wish them to do with your body when you no longer have need of it – burial and where; cremation and disposal of ashes; donation to scientific research.

Those are ways you can take care of your affairs now and genuinely show your concern for those who will do so later. Do it early enough so that no one will have to wonder later if you were competent to do so.

EIGHT

Money Matters

You need to know about your parent's financial resources now, not later, so that you can act on your parent's behalf when it becomes necessary.

You have probably never heard your parent talk about his or her sex life – except, perhaps, with extreme embarrassment during one of those "facts of life" talks you had around the time you achieved puberty.

Our parents' generation was brought up to be extremely reticent about some subjects. They were private matters, not for public discussion. Sex was one of those subjects. Money was another.

I never once heard my father talk about how much he earned, during his working career. Not once. He may have talked about these things with my mother – in fact, I'm sure he did, because they made decisions together, and she maintained the family financial records. But he never mentioned his income to me, or, in my hearing, to anyone else.

We had no idea of his income after retirement, either. We knew he got the usual government pensions. We knew he got a pension from The United Church of Canada, his employer for 40 years, but we didn't know how much. We knew he had bank accounts, but we didn't know where.

We knew he owned his apartment outright, but we had no idea what other investments he might have.

As I indicated in the last chapter, you don't necessarily need to know what's in your parent's will. But you do need to know a lot of other things about your parent's finances. Especially if you're the only child, or the only one who lives close enough to have regular contact with your parent. Because, at various times, you may have to manage those finances.

And that can complicate your relationship with your parent, as well as complicate your life. Make it easier on both of you – find out about those finances now, not later. Don't wait until a crisis of some kind forces your hand, and you have to pry information out of a befuddled and possibly suspicious parent.

Tracing assets

Periodically, Joan and I asked my father to keep us informed about his bank accounts and investments. "We don't want to know how much you have, Dad," we assured him. "We just want to know where you've got it, in case anything happens to you."

That was a euphemism. We didn't want to say, "In case you die suddenly."

So, periodically, he made lists of his bank accounts, his safety deposit box, his life insurance policies, his term investments. He never gave a copy to us, though. He just told us, "You'll find it in the top drawer of the little desk in my bedroom."

After he had to move out of his apartment and into Crofton Manor, we spent several days going through that "top drawer of the little desk." Not to mention the bottom drawer. The tin trunk under the window in his bedroom. The closet in the spare room. And his storage locker in the basement of the building.

Initially, it wasn't to trace his assets. That task came later. Rather, the crisis was income tax time. We needed to find his receipts for charitable donations, medical care, interest and dividend income, pension payments… He was physically incapable of leaving his room in Crofton Manor, too weak to come down to his apartment to help us. He would also have been appalled at the thought of *not* filing, no matter how good his excuse of ill health. To file an income tax return, we had to do the work.

In the process, we found bundles of old letters. Envelopes of old newspaper clippings. Boxes of canceled checks and credit card receipts dating back to the early 1970s. Shoeboxes filled with unidentified photographs.

And we found five – count 'em, *five* – different lists of his assets. He had not dated any of them. We didn't know which one was the most recent. Nor, in his current weakened state, did he. We took them up to him. "I think it's that one," he said. "No, maybe it's, well, no, that's not right, it must be, no…" His voice trailed off, and he slumped back into his bed.

I eventually had to start eliminating lists by trial and error. One of Dad's lists showed an account at the Bank of British Columbia. I took that list to the nearest bank, the Hong Kong Bank of Canada, which had been, in an earlier incarnation, the Bank of British Columbia.

The clerk was very helpful. He checked his computer. "No sir," he said. "That account was closed ten years ago. I can't tell you any more than that, but I can tell you it has been closed for some time."

Scratch that list.

I called a firm listed as holding some of Dad's investments. "That number is no longer in service," a somewhat nasal recording informed me. The telephone book had no firm listed by that name, either. I called a cousin, who had been an accountant until he retired. "I think I remember them," he said. "Weren't they taken over about 15 years ago?"

Scratch another list.

By a process of elimination, I came up with the most recent list. But even it wasn't fully up-to-date. "Yes, that's the one," Dad agreed, when I took it to his room. "But Hopkirk's not my lawyer anymore. He's retired. There's a young man in his firm who's taken over. Nice young man – I wish I could remember his name. And my accountant, he's changed too. Oh, what *is* his name…?"

Eventually, we tracked them all down.

Secrecy or reticence?

I don't think any of this resulted from Dad's wanting to withhold information from me. There's a difference between being secretive and being reticent. Dad spent 20 years of his life as a missionary, overseas – right through the Great Depression back in Canada, right through the Second World War. It was a time when churches had little money. They survived, often, on the sacrifices made by their staff at home and overseas. My parents must have been hard pressed at times. Their poverty was certainly not as great as that of the Indian people living in the gutters and alleys of the city, but not even missionaries could ever have been considered affluent. Others in my father's family were hit harder. Dad's brother Andy, my uncle, had also gone overseas as a medical doctor. While he was home on furlough, the United Church's Mission Board pulled the plug. It no longer had enough money to send him back to India. He ended up having to join the British colonial civil service so that he could continue to serve as a doctor in his beloved India.

Neither Dad nor Uncle Andy ever talked about those hardships. It wasn't done. For the same reason, Dad never discussed his comparative affluence in later years.

Indeed, I'm not sure he actually knew what he had. Financial records, down to the last penny, had been my mother's job. Dad kept his charitable receipts all together in a file folder on a shelf in the closet in his spare bedroom. He had a list of every donation he made. But I found no evidence that he ever added up the total of those charitable donations. He kept meticulous records of checks he had written. But nothing in his checkbook or on his bank statements suggested that he had ever balanced one against the other.

And he definitely did not know how much he had in his bank account when he went into Crofton Manor. He fussed and dithered about writing a check for his initial payment, wondering if he had enough in his bank account to cover it. I checked. He had, at the time, over $20,000 in his account.

It's not unusual, even for famous people, to be confused about their wealth. According to an item in the *Presbyterian Record*, Professor William Barclay, the author of what are probably the world's most widely read commentaries on the New Testament, got worried about his income. The *Record* noted: "He had no real interest in money." A friend had to persuade Barclay to see an accountant. Barclay arrived at the accountant's office with a box "crammed full of bank and royalty statements." Barclay had no idea how well-off he was, financially.

Not everyone has lots of cash available, of course. But not knowing about the state of personal finances seems common. Over and over, when I talked with people about aging parents, they shook their heads in despair as they described how their mother or father had squirreled away this cash here, that bond there. They talked about Savings Bonds that had matured a decade before, about jars of nickels and quarters stashed on pantry shelves. I was told – though I can't corroborate this story – about one mother who for some reason began opening a new account every time she took her annuity check to the bank. Fortunately, an alert teller realized what was happening, and brought the proliferation of accounts under control.

Time for talking

Uncomfortable as it may be, therefore, it's important for you to talk with your parent about his or her finances. Do it while that parent is "of sound mind," because it will be a lot harder to trace things later. You don't want to toss out his lumpy old mattress, and then discover he'd been using it to store $100 bills! Recognize that your efforts may not be welcomed. Depending on what your past relationship has been, your parent may fear that you're planning to take control away from her. Or that you're being too nosy with his assets. Or that you want to use that money for your own purposes.

This is a time for establishing trust, if trust doesn't already exist. Find out about your parent's finances. And then do nothing until you have to. Don't meddle. That's how you show that you're not doing this to rip them off.

Point out, if you have to, that by the time you're down to one parent, it becomes your responsibility to know before it's too late. Because you're the next one who will have to deal with those finances. Don't be put off with promises, or partial information. (I say that, not having done it myself until it was almost too late.) And don't be satisfied with just a list of bank accounts. Find out about pension plan payments, annuities, life insurance policies, and investments of any kind. And then follow up on those contacts, to make sure they are correct.

Not one of my father's lists of assets, for example, included the name of his investment broker. I didn't even know he had one.

"Oh yes," he agreed vaguely, when I asked him about it. "You'll have to get in touch with the man – oh, dash it, what *is* his name? – at Wood Gundy."

Wood Gundy? The name did not appear in anything I had found in his files. I called Wood Gundy. They had no record of my father's ever having an account there. But I *did* find some old statements from Odlum Brown – whom Dad had never mentioned in 20 years. Dad's agent there, Phil Perceval, proved enormously helpful in providing the cash to pay Dad's monthly fees at Crofton Manor.

Find out about liabilities, too. You'll need to know about them eventually, if you become executor.

In the meantime, if your parent becomes incapacitated, for any reason, you may have to make the monthly rental or mortgage payments. You can cancel the telephone and TV cable while your parent's place is vacant, but you'll still have to pay for heat and light and insurance. In the short term, you may be able to cover these costs out of your own resources. But you probably can't afford to do that on a longer term.

Some parents go quite quickly; others may stretch their passing over many years, even decades. Alzheimer's, multiple sclerosis, Parkinson's, ALS, arteriosclerosis – these and other illnesses may disable your parent for extended periods without ever threatening his or her physical survival. Paying for their care out of your pocket could bankrupt you.

Love is not based on economics, you may say. True – and thank God it isn't. But love should not destroy your life either.

If you do pay some of your parent's bills from your own resources, keep financial records as precisely as if you were treasurer for a community organization. Without those records, you'll get nothing back. With them, you may find other family members willing to share the burden, or you may be able to reclaim some costs from the estate, when it is eventually settled.

Alternative financing methods

But what if your parent starts running up massive bills for institutional or medical care? (In Canada, that's not a problem. Most medical care, including expensive surgery, is covered by government plans. In the United States, medical intervention can bankrupt families unless they have private insurance coverage.)

There are two alternatives.

Many elderly people are short of cash. Paradoxically, though, they may have invisible assets locked up in insurance policies, or in their homes.

One reason why the elderly are not likely to move to a new location is that they often have a considerable equity in their homes. Think about it. If you buy a home in your 20s, your mortgage payments may amount to 25 or 30 percent of your income. If you stay in that home, those same mortgage payments some 20 years later will probably be less than 10 percent of your income. By the time you retire, your income may drop drastically, but you'll have no mortgage payments at all – just maintenance and taxes.

In the meantime, though, the value of the home has soared. When Joan and I bought a house in Toronto, in 1968, we paid $28,000 for it. When we sold it, in 1993, in the midst of a drastic real estate slump, we still got $170,000. If we had sold a couple of years earlier, or later, we might have received $100,000 more! Your parents have probably had similar gains on their homes.

Your parent may be able to get what's called a "reverse mortgage" on that increased equity. Your parent takes out a mortgage based on the value of the property, just as one would normally. But instead of *making* monthly payments, your parent *receives* payments. At the time of death, the amount owing is repaid from the sale of the house.

But don't leap at reverse mortgages as a cure-all. They're fairly expensive to set up and restrict the opportunity for a person in the sale of property. For example, if your parent takes out a reverse mortgage on their present house, but then decides to move to some other type of housing, a condominium perhaps, the reverse mortgage would have to be paid off at the time of sale. And if the parent still wants the kind of income a reverse mortgage provides, they would have to negotiate a *new* reverse mortgage, with all the related costs.

The second option is similar to a reverse mortgage, but based on life insurance. Many seniors have significant amounts of life insurance. Some companies – one of the books I read says "hundreds of companies," but I can't personally confirm that – will let your parent draw off "living benefits." That is, part of the proceeds that would be paid out at death can be paid out before death to cover expenses for home care, nursing homes, etc., if the parent is clearly nearing the end.

And, of course, you can buy insurance policies that will pay for home or nursing home care. But only if you buy them in advance. Well in advance. Once your parent needs that care, it's too late. These policies are worth investigating, though I personally consider them a gamble. Premiums tend to be high. For older people, they can be astronomical. After all, insurance companies have to make a profit, so they're going to charge at least as much as they expect to pay out.

Power of Attorney

To pay bills from your parent's accounts, you'll need authority to access them directly. There are two ways of doing it: by Power of Attorney, and by joint account. You'll probably need both.

A Power of Attorney gives you the right to act on behalf of your parent. You may do anything that your parent could do, or would do, if he or she were able to. You can write checks, buy and sell property, buy or sell investments, and enter contracts. In practice, you would do these things only when your parent is incapable of doing them.

But there's a Catch-22 involved here. To be valid, these powers have to be voluntarily granted to you. Which means that your parent has to be mentally competent, both to *give* them and to *withdraw* them. So as soon as your parent becomes mentally incompetent, unable to make those decisions for himself or herself, the Power of Attorney may become invalid. Which is, of course, precisely the moment when you need those powers.

The laws about Power of Attorney vary in every jurisdiction. But here's what happened in British Columbia, when Joan and I granted Power of Attorney to our daughter. Our lawyer drew up a form called an *Enduring* Power of Attorney. That is, a power which will *endure* or continue, even if, for some reason, each of us goes completely *non compos mentis.* Bonkers. Nut cases.

To ensure she doesn't abuse that privilege, our doctor has to certify that in his professional opinion we are no longer capable of managing our own affairs. That could be because of age, or illness. It could also result from a temporary disability, such as a car accident.

But wait, there's more. "You know, if your daughter married the wrong man and they split up, he could use her Power of Attorney to claim half of your assets," our lawyer explained. "You don't want to take that chance, no matter how much you trust her personally. So we name a completely separate third party, to whom you give the power to decide when that Power of Attorney can be invoked. That person has no authority over your assets – none whatever. But he or she decides when you're no longer capable of looking after yourself, and tells your daughter she can start to act on your behalf."

In other jurisdictions, procedures may not be that complicated. But there is almost always some hedge, some qualification. Some states require two medical doctors to certify that your parent is no longer competent. Others require separate documents for financial or real estate transactions.

If you are granted a Power of Attorney, be careful.

First, don't abuse the power you've been given. Don't write checks for your own benefit. That's embezzlement. You were given certain powers to act on someone else's behalf, not for your own personal profit.

Second, don't assume you have powers that you don't actually have. Go to the institutions where you may have to apply those powers, and find out exactly how they will treat you when you come in brandishing your legal papers and expecting things to go smoothly.

Legal matters never run as smoothly as planned. My father anticipated his eventual disability. Ten years ago, he granted me a Power of Attorney, when he first had his heart pacemaker implanted. He wrote me a letter, saying that he had done so. He assumed the letter would be sufficient for me to act on his behalf. It wasn't.

After tracing his bank account, I went to his bank branch with the letter stating that I had Power of Attorney. The bank would not accept it. They required either the original papers, or a notarized copy.

In my experience, banks tend to be much more stuffy about authority than other financial institutions. Insurance companies will often release information about policies, even over the telephone, if you can provide reasonable proof of your right to know. Dad's investment brokers – granted, they knew him well already and had a long history of dealing with him – required only a letter of authorization from me. The trust company handling his annuity payments merely needed some identification to look up his details on their computers. But banks tend to be sticklers for following the rules to the letter.

Dad's lawyer provided the necessary notarized copy of the official Power of Attorney papers. For the next six months, I carried those papers with me everywhere in my briefcase. I had to present them when I went to the Post Office to register his change of address. Without that authority, they wouldn't accept my assurance that he had, in fact, moved. I needed those papers at the bank, when I had to pay bills for him. I needed them again when I renewed his car registration and insurance – even though I thought it unlikely he would ever drive again.

Cover all the bases

But when, after about four months at Crofton Manor, Dad decided he should sell his apartment, I discovered that the papers I had weren't sufficient after all. In British Columbia, apparently, the kind of Power of Attorney that Dad signed was valid indefinitely – except for what's called "real property," that is, real estate. Selling his apartment required a different Power of Attorney, which had to be renewed every three years.

Fortunately, Dad was still quite capable of signing this second Power of Attorney. Otherwise, we would have been stuck. Short of getting a court order authorizing us to act, we could have done nothing about his apartment until after he died, until after letters of probate had been issued and had legally empowered me to act as his executor. And that, as a great many families have discovered, could have gone on interminably. Aging parents can slip into senescence. Their minds flicker and fade, like a candle in a windstorm. They cannot legally act. But their bodies don't know that their minds have gone. And those bodies may still be relatively healthy. They can continue functioning for years and years. Without the proper Powers of Attorney, the family is stuck, having to pay rent or mortgage or upkeep and taxes on a dwelling they cannot dispose of.

I tell you these stories not so that you can anticipate every situation, but so that you can ask the right questions. When does a Power of Attorney come into effect? How and when can it be revoked or canceled? What does it cover? For how long? You don't have to know all the possibilities yourself. Indeed, you probably can't, unless you're a lawyer yourself – and even then there may be regional variations that you're unfamiliar with. Powers of Attorney come under provincial or state law, and therefore every area has slightly different regulations. It pays to work through a qualified lawyer.

An act of trust

Remember that a Power of Attorney is an enormous act of trust on your parent's part. It says, in effect, "I put my life and my possessions in your hands." With an active Power of Attorney, you can do anything that your parent can – in his or her name.

That's an awesome responsibility. One of the Ten Commandments inscribed by Moses after he encountered God on the mountain in the wilderness of Sinai says, in the modern translation of the *New Revised Standard Version*, "You shall not make wrongful use of the name of the Lord your God" (Exodus 20:7). The more historic language of the King James Version says: "Thou shalt not take the name of the Lord in vain."

Having a Power of Attorney enabled me to act in my father's name. If I made "wrongful use of his name," if I abused the privilege he had given me, I would be taking his name in vain. I could damage his reputation; I could harm his credit rating; I could squander his savings. And all in his name.

If, over your lifetime, you have built a good and healthy relationship with your parents, none of these cautions need apply. Your parent trusts you. He or she has confidence in you. And you will reciprocate. You will act responsibly. You will not abuse the privilege granted to you.

If, on the other hand, the adversarial relationships of your teen years have continued into adult life, you can expect some complications. It's possible your father may not trust you enough to put himself into your hands. Or your mother may prefer to give that power to some third party who has no claim on her assets.

Simply put – to be trusted, you had better prove yourself trustworthy. Starting right now. Because granting Power of Attorney is an enormous risk for anyone to take. And I suspect some parents take it only because *not* having a Power of Attorney is an even greater risk.

Still, a Power of Attorney has its limits. It expires, for example, the instant the person dies. At that moment, bank accounts are frozen. So are property ownership, annuity payments, and all kinds of investments. Don't think you can keep on using a Power of Attorney by neglecting to inform the bank, the trust company, or the government. Banks and governments do not take lightly to attempts to do an end run around their rules and regulations – even if, in the end, all of that money would come to you anyway. If they find that you have paid bills using an invalid Power of Attorney, or have accepted payments that should have ceased, you'll have to repay those funds, at best. At worst, you could be imprisoned for fraud or embezzlement.

Joint ownership

An alternative to Power of Attorney is joint ownership. That means both you and your parent legally share ownership. When your parent dies, you become the sole owner of that asset or account. That's a common practice between spouses. Joan and I have joint accounts at all our banks. We've done the same with our house and our cars. If one of us dies, the other will not be hamstrung. The survivor can carry on without complications.

Joint ownership is not as common between children and parents. When it comes to automobiles, for example, depending on where you live and the insurance practices that apply there, if there is an accident, both registered owners might be responsible for damages. If you are worried about your parents' safety behind the wheel in the first place, this may give you extra food for thought.

Joint ownership is probably even less common when it comes to things like financial assets.

I tried to get some of my father's accounts changed to joint ownership, without success. I was given bad advice by a bank financial advisor. Let me amend that – I was given what later turned out to be bad advice. I don't know precisely why this bank officer gave me the advice that he did. When I attempted to get those bank accounts converted to joint ownership, I was still in shock over the role reversal of having a helpless and dependent father. So I'm sure I didn't comprehend everything he told me. Perhaps, at that time and under those circumstances, it was good advice. But in the end, it created far more problems than I needed.

First of all, I discovered that my Power of Attorney was not, by itself, sufficient to change Dad's personal account to a joint account. To authorize the change, my father himself had to come to the bank with me. I drove him downtown to his branch. To this day, I cannot imagine what that drive and visit cost him, in energy and scarce physical resources. He shuffled into the bank leaning heavily on his walker. We sat in those spine-racking chairs that institutions seem to use to make sure customers don't hang around too long. We waited. And we waited. Dad slumped lower and lower in his chair.

Finally we got a young man, nervously hiding behind a desk plaque that called him a "Financial Advisor." We told him what we wanted.

"I think I'd better get my supervisor," he said.

The supervisor came out of his office. I could hear Dad's breath coming in shorter and shorter gasps beside me. He had his eyes closed a lot of the time. I was afraid he might collapse, right there, so perhaps I wasn't listening as closely as I might have in some other circumstances. But the words I recall from the supervisor said something like this: "I don't recommend making it a joint account. If your father died fairly shortly, Revenue Canada might treat it as an attempt to evade taxes by transferring assets on his deathbed, and could reclaim everything."

"What do you recommend, then?" I asked.

"Your Power of Attorney will let you write any checks up until your father's death," he explained. "Are you also his executor?"

"Yes, I am," I replied.

"Then your powers as executor come into effect upon his death. You're covered before and after."

At least, that's how I remember the conversation.

I took his advice. And all I can say now is that he was wrong. I gave the bank a specimen signature, on one of their officious little yellow file cards. The Power of Attorney did, in fact, give me the right to write checks on Dad's account while he was alive. But that power ceased the moment he died. From that moment until the Probate Court approved me as his legal executor, his accounts were frozen, his bank box out of bounds.

After Dad's death, I went into the bank, to find some papers in his bank box. A different young man told me flatly, "I'm sorry. We can't do that."

I was stunned. There was a copy of Dad's will in there. I needed it to prove I was his executor. I needed it to find out what I should do about his estate. His birth certificate was in there. I needed it for the funeral home, so that they could proceed with handling his remains. His insurance policies were in there. Without them, I didn't know who to contact.

Feeling defeated, I started to get up. Like my father, I tend to smother strong feelings. Then I realized how angry I was. "Look," I said, sitting down again and stabbing a forefinger at the startled youth on the other side of the counter. "You guys got us into this – you get us out of it."

He looked bewildered.

I told him my story.

He flushed. He went to check with a supervisor. When he came back, he said, "We're not supposed to do this, but we'll let you check the box and make notes for your information." I actually felt grateful.

"I know what it's like," he commiserated, as we closed Dad's box and locked it away again. "My mother died two years ago."

I came out of that first meeting with representatives of that bank angry and frustrated. "I think we're up shit creek," I told Joan angrily. "We aren't going to be able to get at that box until the will goes through probate, and that could take months!"

In fairness to that particular bank, I have to say that in subsequent meetings, they made an extra effort to make things easier. The representative who originally gave me the bad advice had moved to another branch. Instead, I dealt with Jonathan Pagtakhan – who gave me such excellent service that I think it's worth naming him. The first time I met Jonathan, he looked too young to have graduated from high school, let alone be in management. To this day, I don't know whether he broke rules, bent them, or simply exercised his managerial discretion. Whatever he did, he made everything from then on move smoothly. He found ways to let us access the documents we needed; he helped us list the contents for submission to the Probate Court; he paid the probate fees and the bills connected with the funeral services and cremation out of Dad's account. And he kept us informed, by phone and fax, of everything he did on our behalf.

But none of that would have been necessary if we had had joint ownership in the first place.

I don't recommend spreading joint ownership too widely. Joan and I are not, for example, making our daughter Sharon a joint owner with us of our house, or of our present bank accounts. Not yet, anyway. Because, as our lawyer pointed out, if she married the wrong man and the marriage broke up, we could lose a large portion of our assets. But if one of us should die, the remaining spouse would immediately change many of those assets to joint ownership with her.

Only when necessary

Let me stress, once more, that you need to know about your parent's financial arrangements for one reason, and only one reason – so that you can act on your parent's behalf *when necessary*. Do not try to take over. Do not make your parent feel useless or incompetent. Your parent needs to retain as much independence as possible.

The more that parents can continue to do for themselves, the better off they are. And the better off you are. You're probably under enough emotional stress already – you don't need to take on any unnecessary responsibilities.

Step in only when your parent is incapacitated by illness or senility. Step in only if your parent, left to himself or herself, might make some catastrophic error – such as turning his or her life savings over to a smooth-talking scam artist.

And if your parent recovers, give those responsibilities back. Gladly, and unhesitatingly.

But keep informed, just the same.

Janice Leonard

He lost everything that was familiar

My sister had sole Power of Attorney. She made all the decisions about my father's care; it seemed logical at the time. My parents lived on five acres, and she had the eight acres right next door.

I was away in southern France, in Provence, on a cycling holiday, when she made the decision that my father would have to go into a nursing home. He was 81. It all started when he fell out of a tree. He got a serious head injury in that fall. He was 75, and he had climbed the tree to trim some limbs.

My sister and my mother decided that they should sell the family property. That was very hard, because I had a cottage on it too. My parents had given me that space, to put my own cottage up on. I had no choice in that matter. After it had all been signed, my sister's husband, my brother-in-law, got a brain tumor, and that took all of her energies. So I had to finish off a process that I didn't approve of in the first place, including losing my own cottage.

The hard thing was that I no longer had a place that I could take him for a weekend, when I took him out of the home. It was a familiar place for him to go, and he was so confused, he needed something familiar around him. After the property was sold he lost everything that was familiar to him.

NINE

Accepting
the Reality of Death

Sooner or later, you have to accept the fact that your parent is going to die. Not immediately. But inevitably.

When you direct all of your efforts to keeping your parent alive, and comfortable, it may feel like disloyalty even to think about the possibility of death. It feels like giving up.

When our son Stephen was dying of cystic fibrosis, we – no, *I* – could not acknowledge that reality. To ourselves, or to him. I was afraid that if he ever accepted that his time was limited, he would quit trying to live. I was even more afraid that if *I* admitted it, *I* would quit trying to keep him alive. And I desperately wanted him to live; I could not imagine life without him.

You may have a similar reaction to your parent's mortality. You may not want your parent to die. You may desperately long to have your parent live a little longer – especially if this death seems premature, because of accident or illness. You may want to prolong your parent's life because you can't face the prospect of life without him or her. Or you may feel you need just a little more time to patch up a relationship, to make amends for past feuds, or even to receive a final blessing of some kind.

On the other hand, you may find yourself wishing that your parent would get it over with and pass on to the great beyond, whatever that may be. Your parent may have become a burden, emotionally and financially. The demands of your parent's condition may be driving a wedge between you and your spouse, or you and your children. And you simply don't want to deal with the problems created by your parent's progressive decline.

Both of these reactions derive from the same factor – denial. Denial of death. And worse, denial of dying. I wasn't even able to *say* to anyone else that Stephen was dying until a couple of months before he died. I didn't actually *believe* it until a few days before. Both reactions were too late to help him with his final experiences of life.

Short-term benefits

Denial can have some short-term benefits. Very short-term.

My wife Joan's father had lung cancer. He was diagnosed too late for any hope of surgery or treatment. His condition plummeted. Yet he clung to life until Joan was able to fly across the country to visit him one last time. He rallied while she was there, actually seemed to improve. After she returned to our home in Ontario, he declined rapidly. To keep track of his time in the hospital, he wrote the dates on a tattered brown envelope in a single column. The handwriting remained fairly strong until Joan left. Two days later, it was a spidery scrawl. Three days later, it was illegible.

I think also of a woman I visited in a palliative care ward. I don't remember her name. It might have been Mrs. Powell. I know only that it was part of my responsibilities, during a one-year hiatus in my writing career when I worked for a congregation in suburban Toronto, to visit hospitalized members. The first time I visited her, I thought she was asleep. I sat down by her bed, and held her hand, and talked to her softly. I told her that members of the congregation were praying for her, and cared about her. Her eyes flickered open, briefly. Her fingers, puffed up by her cancer, gave my fingers a barely perceptible squeeze. Her lips mouthed, "Thank you."

On my last visit, a few weeks later, she was propped up by so many pillows she was almost invisible. She had no energy left to do any more than breathe. I got no response at all to my hand, my words – or my tears. I fled from the ward, overcome with despair. I felt that I should be able to *do* something, and there was nothing at all that I *could* do. There was nothing *anyone* could do. She was within a week of death.

But Mrs. Powell hung on through that week, until her daughter's wedding that weekend. Then she let go, and died.

Avoiding the obvious

Denial – a refusal to die based on nothing more than willpower – kept both of these people alive slightly longer. It is possible, by sheer force of will, for aging parents to keep themselves alive for a little longer, until some special occasion, some particular event, has taken place.

But they cannot keep themselves alive indefinitely. All they can do is postpone the end for a short while, because aging parents are gripped by forces larger than they can control. Their bodies, their organs, are breaking down. Whether they accept the reality of death is, ultimately, almost immaterial.

However, acceptance is absolutely crucial for you. Your parent can't delay the inevitable indefinitely. But you can.

You see, if you refuse to accept the realities of dying, of death, you can prevent that aged body from dying. That's a worst-case scenario. Modern medical technology can keep a body alive a long time. Respirators can keep an otherwise dead body breathing. Dialysis equipment can purify the blood. Intravenous drips can provide nourishment. The only thing you can't keep going is the brain – and distraught relatives have been known to refuse to accept a flat line electroencephalograph (EEG) as proof of irreversible death. They insist on continuing what are some-times called "heroic measures." "Mother looks so peaceful," they'll say. "She can't be dead."

Even if you don't go to that extreme, your denial can make the clos-ing days of life miserable for your parent and for yourself by slamming the door on subjects you should have the freedom to discuss. Unless the parent's mind has completely gone – and that's a much smaller percent-age of the population than you might think from a casual visit to most nursing homes – the aging person usually knows that he or she is getting near the end. But your parent won't say so, for fear of offending you. And you won't say so, because you don't want to lose your parent.

And so you go around and around, avoiding the obvious. In his book *The Facts of Death*, Michael A. Simpson referred to this avoidance as "the horse on the dining room table" syndrome. Imagine a dinner party, he suggested, where "a horse is sitting in the middle of the table. But we all talk as if the horse weren't there, for it would embarrass the host if the guests mentioned it at all, and the host doesn't refer to the horse lest it upset the guests. Though it is ignored in the conversation, the horse sits there still, in the center of everyone's thoughts all night."

Too often, we the children want to encourage our parents. We don't want them to give up. And so we persist in saying, "Of course you're going to get better, Mom." Or, "As soon as you're back on your feet, Pop…" The variations on denial are endless: Next summer, we can take a trip back home…; I got your car serviced…; We paid up your mem-berships for next year…; If I got you a computer, we could keep in touch with e-mail messages…

Or else you spend all your time talking about your parent's treat-ment. The pills. The surgery. The diagnosis. The behavior of the nurses or the doctors.

All of these are important. But they miss the main point: "What's going to happen to me? And to everything that's precious to me?" You are the one your parent most wants to talk about these things with. If you refuse to accept the reality of death, you force your parent to submerge these concerns, or to discuss them only with people who can do nothing about them.

So talk with them. If you're an introvert, like me, bring yourself to say the things that you would not normally say, like "I love you." Think about the things that – in the not too distant future – you're going to wish you had said, the questions you'll wish you had asked, and say them, ask them. (If you're an extrovert, learn to ask questions and then just listen!) Of course it will hurt, but it will hurt a lot more, and for a lot longer, to leave these things unsaid. It's part of your healing process.

Healing and curing

Part of our reluctance stems, I suspect, from a confusion between healing and curing. Most parent/child discussions about treatment and medication focus on curing. We don't really expect that parent to grow younger, to go back to the health he or she enjoyed years before. But we want to get rid of, to suppress, those distressing symptoms of increasing age and debility – the intellectual slowing down, the physical weakness, the spiritual depression.

Janet Quinn, Associate Professor and Senior Scholar at the Center for Human Caring, University of Colorado School of Nursing, in Denver, Colorado, helped me grasp the difference between healing and cure.

Healing, she stated in an article in *pmc: the Practice of Ministry in Canada* (September 1997), "remains a mystery. We just know that it is very different from cure."

Contemporary medical curing aims to eliminate the signs and symptoms of disease. We have this multi-gazillion dollar system to eliminate the signs and symptoms. We get rid of the signs and symptoms of disease, but the person is left essentially unchanged.

Heart transplant is the epitome of our modern system. It takes a diseased organ and replaces it with a non-diseased organ. In that moment there is perfect curing – the signs and symptoms of disease have been cut out and replaced. But nothing else has changed in the patient's life. Now, if this person is going to live, he or she needs healing.

People…who go through a crisis…develop a whole new relationship with their family from whom they've been estranged for years. Or they come into a whole new relationship with God. They come into an awareness that they are loved, actually loved. This to me is the miracle of healing.

Healing may occur without curing.

Curing may or may not be possible, because it is limited to the body physical. Healing is *always* possible. Even as the body gets sicker and sicker, the person as a whole can continue to unfold.

Learning a bit from experience

Quinn concludes with a question: "Everybody will die. But will everybody die knowing that they are loved?"

As aging parents reach the end of their lives, they need, more than anything else, to know they are loved. That is the most healing thing they can experience at this stage. If you reject the reality that your parents are going to die, you may well deny them the healing that they need.

"I wish someone had told me this, when I was losing my father," says Bonnie Schlosser, president of Northstone Publishing and publisher of this volume. "We were so busy just trying to get him through it, and to get us through it, that we didn't take the time to contemplate, to talk with him. I wish someone had taught me how to raise these subjects, how to recognize his cues to us…"

Because I wasn't able to accept that she was dying, I was no help to Mrs. Powell. With the typical North American obsession with physical action, I couldn't see that simply *being* there with her might be enough. Just to keep her company for a while, in her last days. But I didn't see that as *doing* anything *useful*.

I wasn't much help to my mother, either. During that last week of her life, we never admitted to her, or to ourselves, that she was dying. Dad said, as we left the hospital two hours before she died, "You know, I think she's breathing a little better tonight."

But she knew. The first day I got there, she told me what she wanted done with her collections of china: "The red dinner set goes to Ruth Fawcett. I want you to have that blue and gold serving dish, for Joan. The blue dinner set is for…"

I nodded, and tried to remember. But my emotions kept saying to me, "She'll get better, and be able to write all of this out for you. You don't need to do anything about it. Not yet." If I had been able to admit to myself that my mother was dying, that this might be our last chance to talk about these things, I could have been more helpful to her.

Fortunately, by the time my father's turn came around, I had learned not to deny the reality of death.

Too weak to recover

It started with a simple cough. The lung congestion resulting from his weakened heart function made it worse. After we moved him from his apartment into Crofton Manor, it got even worse – perhaps a reaction to a new environment that, while he may have agreed to, he didn't really want to be in.

Crofton Manor called me at my home one Friday morning to say that they had just sent Dad back to hospital. I started driving down to Vancouver. Barely six hours after the phone call, I pulled into the hospital's parking lot. I found Dad in Ward 2A. He was almost too weak to greet me.

As I watched, another paroxysm of coughs hit him. It wouldn't stop. He had no energy to cough with, but still the coughs doubled him up, folded him over, clutching his convulsing gut. When it finished, he fell back on the pillow, totally exhausted. Other spasms were so severe they made him throw up a vile reddish fluid; they gave him nosebleeds; they left him sobbing helplessly.

On the Saturday morning, he decided he would rather die than go on this way. One of the nurses came around with medication.

"I don't want it," Dad said.

"Oh, but you have to keep trying," the nurse encouraged him.

A spasm of coughing hit him. Two other nurses came in to help him get over it. When it eventually stopped, Dad whimpered, "I'm too tired to keep trying."

It sounded like a wish.

When we were alone, I took him in my arms. He used to be about my size and weight. Now he was a bag of bones inside a sack of loose skin, skin that hung in folds like a plucked chicken's. I held him tight, and gave him permission to die. I whispered, "Dad, if you want to go, if it's time to go, it's okay. You don't have to hang on for me."

He burst into tears. It felt like a relief. "I want to go," he blubbered. "I want to go now."

Permission to die

Over and over, in talking with others who are struggling to cope in one way or another with aging parents, they tell me, "I think he/she really wants to die…"

And I ask, "Have you given them permission?"

They look startled. It apparently hasn't occurred to them their parent might be waiting for approval from them, the children.

This is the ultimate reversal of roles. As infants, we needed our parents' support to live. Now our parents need our permission to die.

Let's be clear about two things.

First, giving permission does not mean encouraging your parent to die. Or assisting them to die. Or abandoning them to die. It just means that they don't have to hang on for your sake. They're your parents – they've probably spent a lifetime trying to protect and nurture you. Even now, on their deathbeds, they will still try to protect you from pain and suffering. So if they sense that you still want them, still need them, to sustain your life, they will try to deny death, right up to the very end. And if they never receive your permission, they may die feeling that they have failed you.

Second, giving permission is not the same thing as wanting your parent to die. It's not like saying, "Aw, drop dead, Mom!" That's an act of denial, not of acceptance – denial of both the person and the relationship. It denies any possibility of healing and reconciliation.

At some point when you were growing up, your parents gave you permission to leave home, to live your own life independent of them. They didn't know how you would do it, or when you would do it, or what your new life would mean for them. But they did it with love, knowing it was best for you. Now, you're doing the same thing for your parents. They need permission to move on. And you don't how it will happen, when it will happen, or what it will mean for you. But you, too, do it with love.

My father did not, in fact, die as soon as I gave him permission. There was no question about his desire to die. Later, during the day, he confirmed that wish to the resident doctor, to his day nurse, and to his night nurse. When his friend Bernice Balfour visited late in the afternoon, he told her too: "It's time. I've waited long enough."

An extended coughing spasm racked him that evening. He ended with a series of grunts: "Now. *Now!* NOW!"

But it didn't work that way. You can't *will* death – you can only accept it.

He was as helpless as a baby. He could barely raise an arm. He couldn't roll over in bed by himself. The mind that used to love a philosophical argument had virtually shut down. When his bladder filled, he needed help using the urinal. He was too weak to fumble his penis into the neck of the urinal. I had to help him. In biblical times, it was an offense for children to see their father that way – naked, exposed.

I asked his doctor about his chances of recovery. We stood out in the hall, where we could talk without Dad overhearing. The doctor said, "To tell the truth, I doubt if he's ever going to come out of hospital. He's too weak. He just hasn't the strength to get better."

Night watch

Such situations evoke incredibly powerful emotions. After my father said it was time to go, I held his head on my shoulder. I don't know that I have ever felt such tenderness towards another person – certainly not since our children were babies, and I held them the same way.

However, I misunderstood how soon the end would come. I attributed to a very sick man an awareness, a prescience, that he was simply not capable of. So I believed he would die that day. Or that night.

I didn't want him to die alone. I didn't want him to open his eyes in his last moment in life and feel that he had been left to die alone, like an animal crawling into a cave to die. So a small group of us – his friend Bernice, his grandniece Sue Brouse, and I – arranged to sit with him in shifts, around the clock.

I had the fewest outside commitments, so I took the night shift. His night nurse found me a recliner chair. Throughout the ward, the lights began to go out. The wards settled into silence – although there is really no such thing as silence in a hospital ward.

In the darkness, I timed the periods between Dad's coughing fits. I couldn't read my watch in the blackness, so I counted seconds. I don't recall him having any period of rest longer than 90 seconds. Sometimes he just had to clear his throat. Sometimes he forced out a few barks. Several times an hour, he had coughing attacks. Each time, I struggled out of the recliner, fumbled through the dark to his bed, and cradled his convulsing body in my arms. I rubbed his back, his chest, his neck, trying to find the key spot that might click off the trigger making him cough. I stroked the thinning hair that clung to his tight scalp. I kissed his forehead.

It occurred to me, as I sat with him in the darkness, counting the seconds between spasms, that all that anyone really has, in the end, is relationships. Nothing else matters. Nothing else survives.

Most of us spend our lives accumulating things. Toys, when we're younger – and often as adults too. Titles of various kinds, occupational and honorary. Positions, voluntary and professional, that give us some social status, and sometimes some power. Physical strength and stamina, to make us self-sufficient. Possessions of many kinds – books and china, furniture and cell phones, computers and paintings…

But when life winds down, none of these can comfort us. When you lie in a bed, too weak to use muscles anymore, too tired to speak, then all those toys and titles, positions and possessions, fade into insignificance. All that matters is relationships. Who cares enough about you to come and sit there, just to be with you?

Through the crisis to the other side

So I sat with him. One night. Two nights. The third night, he whispered, with a voice almost unrecognizable as his own, "I think I'm through the crisis. I'm going to be okay."

I wanted to believe it. But I couldn't. I didn't think it was possible for anyone to slip so far down and still come back.

But towards the end of that third night, I realized that I had slept – uneasily, but for over an hour. Dad was still coughing every few minutes, but not as badly. And he was breathing through his nose again, not gasping through his mouth. He had even rolled onto his side. Without help.

Outside Dad's hospital window, the sky changed imperceptibly from pitch black to dull gray, to pale pewter. The pair of fir trees outside the window gradually separated themselves from the night. They became distinct, three-dimensional, real.

Dawn had come. Life had returned. For the time being, at least.

It was my father's 93rd birthday.

Incredibly, he continued to improve during the following months. Given his weakened state, it took a long time. It took him almost two months just to recover his voice. Shaping words past chronic laryngitis took enormous effort. We hesitated to ask him questions; his attempts to answer required expenditures of energy that he didn't have available.

Signs of improvement

That's something else you have to learn – usually the hard way. Accepting the reality of death doesn't mean making it happen. Acceptance may simply introduce a kind of courtship ritual, a mating dance, between your parent and death. Death comes close, and backs off; brushes a cheek, and hides; rushes in, and withdraws. It may take weeks, months, even years, to consummate the union.

I confess that I felt a bit cheated when my father began to recover. Partly, I suppose, I felt that my sacrifices of the last few days had been wasted. More likely, I feared that I might have to go through the same sacrifices again and again... I almost wanted it over and done with.

The record of my long distance telephone calls between March and August tells the tale of his recovery. At first, no calls lasted more than a couple of minutes. Gradually, as his speech and some energy returned, the calls got longer. By August, much to my surprise, our final telephone conversation ran 14 minutes.

When he first returned to Crofton Manor, the staff brought a wheelchair to take him to and from the dining room. The first sign of his returning vitality came when he refused to use the wheelchair. "I can get myself to the dining room," he rasped. "It's good for me to get the exercise." He used his walker, slowly, painfully, shuffling himself down the hall.

By July, he had set the walker aside. He didn't use it at all. He used a cane. By August, he often forgot to take his cane with him

In April, I tried to find subjects that would stimulate him, that would get his mind going again. "There isn't much intellectual stimulation here," he had lamented.

"There's at least as much as you'd have had in your apartment," I protested.

But he wasn't interested in being reasonable. He wanted sympathy, not argument.

During June, he repeated his complaint.

"Well, you know, the gatherings you used to go to moved around to various people's homes," I suggested. "There's no reason they couldn't come to you here, if you can't go to them."

He took my suggestion seriously – an indication of his improved physical and mental condition. "That's true," he admitted. "But my room isn't big enough for more than a couple of people."

"You could book one of the lounges," I continued.

That was a new thought. "I wonder who I'd ask about that?" he pondered. "Perhaps the head nurse would know."

The gift of time

But neither of us ever forgot how close he had come to death. Several times, as I simply sat in his room, reading a book or a magazine while he watched World Cup Soccer matches on TV, or worked on a crossword puzzle, he looked up and said, "You know, I should have died back there in the spring."

"I know," I replied.

"I can't understand why God is still keeping me here," he added.

A friend and fellow-writer, Diane Forrest, helped me understand why. I was in Toronto, on a business trip, and got together with Diane for lunch. I was sounding off about the process of dying. About how long it took. About how much I hated to see my father reduced to a helpless wreck. "Why does dying have to be such a miserable business?" I demanded.

Diane had lost her mother a couple of years before. "Because it gives us time to make friends with our parents," she replied.

Her father, Al Forrest, had been my boss, years before. He had died suddenly and unexpectedly. He woke early one morning. Rather than disturb his wife by tossing around in bed, he got up and went into his living room to read a book. That's where his family found him, several hours later, the light on behind his chair, spilling down over his shoulder, over the book he still held in his hand.

He left everything unfinished. There were no goodbyes, no instructions, no last wishes, no patching up of quarrels or misunderstandings.

By contrast, my father and I had time to deal with some of that unfinished business. To tie up some loose ends of his life. To let him write out, in a spidery and trembling hand, some thank you notes to distant relatives and overseas acquaintances. To let him move towards closure.

I asked him what kind of memorial service he would like, when the time came.

"Nothing special," he said. "Just a regular service. Nothing sentimental or soppy."

"How about hymns?" I asked.

He thought about that for a minute. "*Guide Me, O Thou Great Jehovah*," he said at last. "We sang that one at Mary's service. It's always been one of my favorites. And maybe a metrical psalm from the old Scottish Psalter – Chris loved them."

"What do you want done with your ashes?" I asked him, on another occasion. Both of his wives – my mother and Chris Fraser – had been cremated. Dad had scattered their ashes under trees planted in their name at a memorial garden in North Vancouver.

"I don't really care," he shrugged. "I won't be around."

"Do you want them with Ma's and Chris's ashes?" I persisted. "I wondered if you would like them scattered on one of your fishing rivers somewhere."

"I don't really care," he repeated.

But later that week, he sent me a note. By mail. In a tiny, cramped script obviously written with great difficulty, he told me, "Until you asked, I hadn't thought at all about my ashes. Since then, I have been thinking about it. And I think I would like to have my ashes scattered on the Skagit River, if possible. It's always been the favorite of all my fishing rivers, and I'd like to be part of it when I go."

We could not have had those conversations, if both of us had not faced, and accepted, the reality of his coming death.

Carolyn Terry

I could have denied death a better way

I was really unwilling to accept my dad's aging and dying, and I didn't want to believe it would happen. I used to give him little pep talks about people I heard about who lived past 100. Once he mentioned that I might inherit a bit of money if it didn't all get used up by nursing home care, and I blurted, "I'd rather have you than *any* amount of money."

I was denying that he'd ever change or get weaker or die.

I can't bear the deaths of people I love. I want to deny death. But I should have denied death in a better way, by talking to Dad about what life after death would be like, and by making him promise to meet me when I die.

Maybe I could have dealt better with his weakening, if I hadn't seen it as the beginning of the end of our relationship.

❧

David Keating

The effort it takes just to sit with someone who's dying

Dad died Christmas Day at home.

The hardest part, I think, is the gnawing sense of disloyalty, even betrayal, that accompanies the feeling that caring for Dad was a "drain." Didn't he and Mom take the time to teach me, well, everything? How to walk, to talk, to feed myself. How can I even think of the relatively short period of time I gave him as a drain?

Let me be clear. I would not trade the experience of this time, regardless of its inevitable conclusion, for anything in the world. Nevertheless, I believe that if we deny or minimize the effort that it sometimes takes just to sit with someone who is dying, we lie. We leave ourselves wide open to becoming exhausted and resentful. We unconsciously throw up barriers to those feelings, and distance ourselves from our parent or other loved one at the very time when it is most important to draw close.

Dad and I often reminisced about things we had done together. It might have been a customer in our welding business, or the Father's Day when we paddled a canoe around the island I had grown up on – 26 miles on a sunny day, and two days later Dad ended up with lips so badly sunburned that we were scared he had lip cancer.

When we take such trips down memory lane with an old friend, or a former classmate, it makes for a warm and energizing evening. This was different. I often left Dad's bedroom, sometimes after only a few minutes, feeling torn apart, wrung out. Maybe because we weren't going to be telling these stories to each other much longer, and we both knew it.

A friend who practices Therapeutic Touch once told me that it takes a lot of energy to die. It was her way of describing what she felt when working with the terminally ill, and reflected her understanding of us as existing within a universal flow of energy. While I may not accept all of her ideas, the possibility that I felt drained because I was offering some little strength to Dad comforts me.

੨੭

TEN

When Hope Ends

Few people with a dying parent can avoid at least thinking about euthanasia – if for no other reason than as a powerful incentive to obey the Golden Rule.

When an airliner starts taxiing down the runway for takeoff, there comes "a point of no return." Beyond that point, the pilot can no longer abort the takeoff and still come safely to a stop before running out of runway.

When an elderly parent starts down the long slide towards death, there also comes "a point of no return." Past a certain point, there is no longer any hope of that person recovering "normal" life – whatever that may be at his or her age.

"Normal" is hard to define. For your parent, life has already narrowed down drastically. Your mother rarely leaves her room; your father can no longer communicate. They can't quilt or do woodwork; they have trouble reading; they complain of recurring pain. Nevertheless, they may still enjoy and value their relationships with you, with their friends, with their grandchildren.

On the other hand, your parent may sit idly all day, waiting for death. He has said all the goodbyes that he's ever going to say; she has made all the efforts at reconciliation that she can. These parents may have gone already – they just haven't died physically yet.

In either situation, a cold, an ear infection, or a bout of diarrhea may debilitate them further. But these maladies can be treated. In time, parents with those maladies can recover most of their former capacities. On the other hand, if life is no longer worth living, is it worth bringing them back once more from a fever? Is it worth resuscitating them after a heart attack?

And finally, what of the parent who slips into a coma, or who spends endless days and nights in pain? Once an aged parent enters a vegetative state, the chances of recovery apparently drop below 5 percent. A parent with terminal cancer may require morphine, day and night, to keep pain under control. In such cases, the patient is often better off at home or in a palliative care hospice than in a hospital, because hospital staff sometimes have such a fear of contributing to potential addiction that they're reluctant to prescribe enough of the narcotic. It's an irrational fear. Addiction rarely results from the use of narcotics for genuine pain relief – when the pain abates, so does the need for the narcotic. Family members and palliative care workers don't usually fear addiction; their primary concern is almost always the comfort of their parent or patient.

But as pain or helplessness progress, past the point of no return, the question arises about helping the dying person along. In short, euthanasia.

Levels of care

When is enough, enough?

When we first took my father to Crofton Manor, we were asked to sign a medical directive about the levels of care we wanted him to have. There were basically four levels:

1. Do nothing but keep the patient comfortable.
2. Treat illnesses and accidents with external applications and oral medicines only.

3. Hospitalize as necessary, for intravenous medication and feeding, surgery if appropriate, but do not resuscitate, and take no extraordinary measures such as respirators, transplants, or intensive care.
4. Take any and all measures necessary to prolong or restore life.

We were able to eliminate the first and last options fairly quickly. We didn't want Dad hooked up to a lot of tubes, being kept alive by technology when he would rather slip away. But neither did we want him finished off by a common cold when some commonsense treatment could let us enjoy his company for a while longer.

After considerable discussion among the four of us – Joan, Sharon, me, and Dad, whenever he was able to participate – we opted for level three, because he had been, up to that time, enjoying quite good health for his age. He was living independently, taking part in church and community activities, driving his own car, visiting friends, and carrying on all the normal daily activities of people much younger than himself. While we didn't really expect him to return to his apartment and live on his own again, we did hope he would recover enough to resume many of his hobbies and interests.

That feeling, I found in my interviews, was common among many children looking after their parents. One couple kept a weaving loom for years, expecting their mother would get back to using it. Another kept the family car garaged for six years. No one wants to close doors too soon.

Emotional roller coaster

Our expectations fell short, but I don't think our choice of care level was wrong. Despite repeated (and frustrating) trips into hospital, Dad did get better over the following months. A lot better.

That's one of the facts of life one has to learn about elderly people, sometimes painfully. They rarely slide smoothly and predictably into death. Like a stone skipped across the surface of a lake, they tend to sink and rise, sink and rise, many times. Their health goes up and down like the stock market. About the time you give up hope, they start to recover. And just as you're ready to celebrate their improvement, they crash again. The down turns are precipitous; the climb back up is long and slow. And the older the person, the steeper the plunge, the slower the recovery.

I realized, when I looked back, that we had been going over this roller coaster of emotions for at least three years, ever since friends and former colleagues threw a 90th birthday celebration for Dad. They sent out invitations, booked caterers, arranged for speeches.

Dad almost didn't go to his own birthday party. He came down with some kind of cold or flu. With his heart condition, even a minor cold had serious effects. He said he didn't approve of the party, anyway. "I don't see any point in celebrating mere chronological longevity," he grumbled. On the day of the party, February 23, 1995, he didn't feel any better.

But as usual, he yielded to duty. He got dressed up in his best suit. "I'll make an appearance," he assured us. "But I'm going to leave early."

He didn't. Once he started meeting the 150 or more friends and associates who had come to wish him well, he started enjoying himself. He was surrounded by animated discussion. He shook hands; he chatted; he glowed. He enjoyed himself so much that we had trouble dragging him away from his conversations to the cake-cutting ceremony. By the time we got him into the room to blow out 90 candles, they had melted into a large blue puddle, rippling across the icing and dripping down the sides.

But that party exhausted him. The flu or cold or whatever it was lasted almost a year. We didn't think he would ever regain his strength. Then, just as we were starting to think we should plan for his funeral, he recovered. Not fully. But over the next two years, he took a Mediterranean cruise, and a trip across Canada to the Maritime Provinces and Newfoundland.

Just when he looked as if he would continue for several more years, he had those two heart attacks in January 1998. He went down further than he had ever been before, before he started back up again.

But that summer, I discovered, he was getting engaged in the debate over the United Church's role in residential schools. Several of his younger ministerial colleagues thought that the church had done wrong, and should apologize and make reparations, with no strings attached. Dad didn't defend the behavior of those who had abused their students, sexually, physically, or emotionally. But he argued that the people involved in the residential schools were not necessarily evil. Most of the people in these schools were highly committed Christians, doing what they believed best according to the values of their time. He felt it unfair to judge their actions, and the schools, by standards that didn't exist at the time.

Two months before, that kind of passion would have been impossible. He wouldn't have had the energy.

Acts of closure

A week before his death, Dad was walking without either cane or walker.

He had repeatedly urged Joan and Sharon to come to Vancouver with me, to go through the things in his apartment before it was sold, to decide who wanted which pieces of furniture or china or books. He accompanied us to the apartment three times. We wanted him to rest, but he kept getting up and wandering around and telling us about this piece of furniture or that photo album.

On the Sunday morning, he was well enough to come with us to worship at his home church, for the first time in six months. He had said, earlier, that he really missed going to worship. It was part of the "lack of intellectual stimulation" that he had lamented.

The next day, Sharon and Dad returned to his apartment once more, while Joan and I drove back to the Okanagan. He gave Sharon all his fly-fishing gear, one piece at a time. With each rod, each reel, each group of flies, he told her how it had come to him, where he had used it, what it was particularly good for... Now and then, he'd interrupt himself, and ask, "Can I give you another bit of advice?"

It was, I think, a form of closure for him.

Second thoughts

Without the level of care we had arranged for him to have, he would not have had that final opportunity.

But I have to confess, there were times when I wondered if we had done the right thing. We knew any improvement in his health could only be temporary. At his age, he could not expect very much more time – at best, another year or two. Simply because he was mortal, his health would inevitably decline again.

None of us wanted him to die, of course. We all knew that when he did die, his absence would leave an enormous void in our lives. Yet death meant a bigger loss for him than for us. We would lose just one person; he would lose everyone. But he was ready to die.

And there were several times when I wished that he *could* die, that a body that had spent 93 years trying to survive would give up the struggle and let him go. He had no fear of death. If anything, he was calmly confident. He didn't know what was coming, but he had no doubts that he would be welcomed somehow into God's presence. That was enough for him.

I spent a fair amount of time inside those hospital wards while my father was in and out of the hospital. There were a lot of hopeless cases there.

In one ward, the man in the next bed had lost control of both his body and his mind. He said only two intelligible things, both expletives: "Oh shit!" and "God-damn." During the days, he mostly just moaned; during the nights, he whimpered.

His wife visited him every afternoon. It was the only time he got out of bed each day. The nurses got him up, put him into a dressing gown, and strapped him into a chair. Without the straps, he slowly tipped over, like a Tim Conway comedy skit, and toppled onto the floor.

His wife sat beside him and tried to feed him soup, stew, whatever.

"How long has he been like this?" I asked.

"About a year," she said. "I come in every day at this time."

"Is there any hope for improvement?"

"None. It's just his age." She choked up. "He can only get worse."

Down the hall, a woman wrapped in a quilt sat in a wheeled commode and moaned endlessly, "Help me. Help me. Somebody please help me…"

Around the corner, an Italian family clustered around their patriarch, having the equivalent of a picnic lunch. They alternated between boisterous laughter and agonized wailing, while the gaunt old man lay motionless on his pillows.

If that sounds like a hospital from hell, it wasn't. The facilities were excellent. The quality of nursing was outstanding. Without exception, the staff treated their patients with kindness, caring, and compassion. I never heard any nurse lose her patience, with anyone.

Evidences of love

Sometimes, when sitting with Dad felt like emotional overload, I got up and walked the halls. Through open doors, I heard fragments of conversation. "You were the best mom in the world," said one. Another: "Tomorrow, maybe we can get a wheelchair, and take you for a walk. Would you like that?"

Over and over, I heard people caring when there was no hope for improvement. Logically, they should just have let their loved ones go. There was nothing more that could be done for them. And often, the parent didn't want anything done for them. Like my father, they were ready to go. They *wanted* to go.

I'm still not sure how much of a favor we did my father, or any of those dying persons, by keeping them alive. If Dad could have asked me for help, at his lowest point, it would have been for help to die, not to live.

I shocked the nurses when I asked, "Isn't there some way we can just turn off his pacemaker?"

Dad had had pacemaker problems the previous Thanksgiving, while visiting us at home. We rushed him into Kelowna General Hospital. I stood and watched one morning, while the cardiologist adjusted the pacemaker's rhythms. Faster. And slower. And, for about 20 seconds, off. Dad's eyes, drooping sleepily, suddenly popped wide open. He knew something had happened. But I saw no terror, no fear. And there was no pain. If he had to go, it would have been a good way.

But short of suffocating him with his pillow, I could not help him die. Nor could the medical staff. I was as helpless as he was.

Here and there, I hear that doctors and nurses are not prepared to stand by helplessly anymore. In Canada's most publicized case of euthanasia, Sue Rodriguez apparently died of a drug overdose provided by a sympathetic but unknown doctor. I don't endorse Dr. Kevorkian's "assisted suicide," although I understand and sometimes even sympathize with his motivation.

Yet I know that I could not have suffocated my father with a pillow. I desperately wanted to end his suffering, but I could not have taken the step of ending it for him. Not with the pillow. Not with an injection. Because I loved him, and I didn't want to lose him – even if he was far from the man I held dear in memory.

No one with an aging parent, a dying parent, can avoid at least thinking about euthanasia. My friend David Bryson put it this way after his father's death:

I think there is a kind of continuum between murder and mercy killing. Here in Halifax, Dr. Nancy Morrison was tried for killing a patient. I gather that there is not much doubt that she administered a lethal dose of painkiller, or instructed someone else to administer such a dose. But that was not murder. This was a case where nothing was working, where the patient was in the worst pain anyone in that hospital had ever seen. I do not recommend or endorse euthanasia, but I think there should be something within the realm of a physician to terminate a life that has nothing at all left. When a person has nothing left to live for, there is no reason to prolong that life.

My dad was not able to speak at the end, but he was able to communicate the fact that he was ready to go. It might be nice to have me visit for an hour, but there were still 23 hours left when he was on his own, with little or nothing to live for. It never crossed our minds to advocate euthanasia in Dad's case, but I can be sympathetic to the idea of medical euthanasia when someone has lived their full life and clearly wants to let go.

When people become inconveniences

The usual fear of euthanasia is that it will give carte blanche to those who would like to get rid of inconveniences – especially if those inconveniences have money to pass along to their heirs. I don't agree. Perhaps there are people who think so little of their parents. All I can say is, I haven't met them. Not in that hospital ward. Not in the halls or the waiting lounges. Not at Crofton Manor. And while the interviews I did may not be a true sample of the population at large, I heard nothing that indicated any of people I talked to would arbitrarily end the life of someone they loved.

Perhaps those who consider their aged or ailing relatives an inconvenience don't bother showing up at a hospital. All I know is that from what I saw and heard, both patients and family members would treat euthanasia only as a last resort. And then it would be an act of mercy, not of convenience.

The risk with euthanasia, it seems to me, is not from individuals but from systems. From governments, and social agencies, and organizations, and corporations. They're composed of individuals, and they exist to serve individuals, but no matter how lofty their original goals, after a while they tend to treat those individuals as a means to an end. The institution's own priorities – anything from working more efficiently to balancing the budget – start to take over. And individuals soon become sacrificed for the cause.

I don't think I'm being unduly harsh in that judgment. Over the last two decades, there have been ample examples. Corporations have tried to fatten their profits by sacrificing their most loyal employees. Governments have slashed their deficits by withdrawing funding from those who can least afford food and medical care. In Canada's tainted blood scandal, the Red Cross chose to protect its reputation and its operating budgets rather than the safety of those receiving blood products.

Systems do not develop personal relationships. Rather, they treat individuals as ciphers in the database, cogs in the machine. For that reason, bureaucrats and administrators, let alone governments, should be the last people to have the power to decide about euthanasia. It was, after all, the legitimately elected government of Alberta, here in Canada, that as late as the 1970s sterilized about 3,000 people who were considered mentally deficient, to prevent them from reproducing. Some of those sterilizations were for cerebral palsy, which is usually the result of birth trauma, not genetics; others were for maladies as common as chronic depression, which is now fully treatable.

A system becomes a mindset. It can too easily rationalize the elimination of some for what it considers to be the benefit of the larger group. That was the basis of Hitler's Holocaust in Germany, or of Mao Tse-tung's efforts to exterminate artists and intellectuals in China.

I don't trust systems. Without personal relationships, unknown administrators poring over their balance sheets could well decide that all sick people over 80 were a detriment to community well-being. A province or state might decide to abort all Down's syndrome fetuses as a drain on medicare. Medical insurance plans might decide it was more cost effective to do away with victims of Parkinson's disease, or Huntington's chorea, or ALS (commonly known as Lou Gehrig's disease) rather than provide long-term care. A system comes to these decisions to protect itself, to ensure its own survival. They're what any sensible person would do (indeed, would have to do) if charged with responsibility for the system. But the system is paramount, not those it serves.

It's not hard to come to such conclusions if your goals are efficiency, or profit, or – in Hitler's Germany or Milosevic's Serbia – racial purity.

Responsible relationships

I won't pretend that individuals always act rightly. Lots of aging parents have been exploited and abused by their children. Ann Landers' advice column seems to carry at least one of these stories every week. Children have mismanaged their parents' finances and left them broke. Some have deliberately exploited a Power of Attorney or joint account to rob their parents – especially if those parents are no longer mentally competent to keep track of their own affairs.

But individuals, if they harm their parents or other relatives, do it for predictable motives. They don't rationalize their cruelty away with lofty intentions.

That might sound like cold comfort. But at least you know what to expect.

Now bear with me, please, because I know I'm going to have trouble getting this thought across. People whose intelligence I respect read an early draft of this chapter, and misunderstood me. So I'm going to try again.

Suppose you're 84, in poor health, but still clear in mind most of the time. You can still enjoy relationships with your children and grandchildren – but you get tired more quickly than you used to. You're in a care facility of some kind. And you're costing the facility, or the government, or an insurance company, a lot of money.

One day, your condition crosses over a fine line of some kind, and you become expendable. Maybe your treatment costs go up by 37 cents a day, but that's 23 cents more than a corporate guideline. Or you have a birthday, which puts you over a critical age. Or you doze for more than, say, 15 hours and 42 minutes a day – an arbitrary figure some group of faceless experts somewhere has defined as the boundary line between conscious and comatose. The next thing you know, someone comes in and starts administering a lethal dose of morphine.

Would you say, with tolerant resignation, "I guess they must know what they're doing"?

I wouldn't. Because those decisions about my life all come from people at a distance, people who don't know me, don't care about me, and who have no accountability to me. I may have voted for a political party, or for a specific political candidate, but not for that policy. I had no say in choosing the directors of the corporation, nor did I have any input into the medical guidelines.

I have become simply a number.

If I'm going to put my life in someone else's hands, I want it to be someone I know. Someone whose reactions I can, to some extent, predict. An individual. A specific person. Not an anonymous analyst poring over statistics in a cubicle far away, or a preening politician seeking re-election in a caucus chamber behind closed doors.

At least I'm dealing with a relationship I know about.

Living the Golden Rule

This is where the explanation gets difficult. Please don't misunderstand me.

I am not arguing that parents reap what they sow – although there is some truth to that maxim. I am not simply suggesting that parents will get what they deserve. Rather, I'm arguing that euthanasia offers perhaps the most profound illustration of the Golden Rule: "Do unto others as you would have them do unto you."

It's true, of course, that good parents can have bad kids, and vice versa. Some parents and children don't get along. They never have. Usually, they both know it. They both know that there has been a breakdown of trust, of respect, and certainly of love. I'm not laying blame here. I'm merely stating what should, to my mind, be obvious – by the time old age rolls around, the way children will treat their parents should not come as a complete surprise. It may be too late for those parents to change that relationship with their children.

But it's not too late for you to affect your relationship with your children – by the example you show them of how you behave with your parents. That's my point.

In his book *What Are We Going to Do Now?* author William Molloy recounts a story told by the Brothers Grimm, but it probably goes back much further into folklore. A couple had taken their elderly father into their home. His behavior constantly offended the young couple. His hands shook, so he slopped his soup bowl on their good dining room table. He drooled. He spilled gravy on the wife's place mats. They scolded him. They tried to train him to make less of a mess. Nothing worked. To protect their possessions, they refused to let him sit at the table with them. They gave him his own little table. In the corner. Behind the stove, right out of their way.

They didn't have to watch him embarrassing them anymore. But he dropped her good Royal Doulton china. He broke her Waterford crystal glasses. So they gave him something he couldn't break. A wooden bowl and a wooden spoon. For his own good, of course.

One day, the couple noticed their young son chipping at an old piece of lumber with his pocket knife.

"What are you doing, son?" they asked.

"I'm making a wooden spoon for you and Daddy to eat with when you grow old," the son replied proudly.

As Molloy told that story, the couple came to their senses. The old man was immediately reinstated to the dining table. That strikes me as a Hollywood happy ending. It presumes that a relationship can change in a single instant, and stay changed.

For me, the real point of the story is not a happy ending, but the son's comment. The way the couple treated the old man was the way their son was prepared to treat them.

Let's paraphrase the Golden Rule: "As you do to your parents, so will your children do to you."

If you treat your parents with contempt or disgust, your children will learn that attitude from you. If you rip off your parents, they'll be more likely to rip you off when it's your turn. And if you use euthanasia to hasten your parents out of this world, you might as well expect your children to do the same for you.

Euthanasia becomes a self-liquidating problem.

At the personal level

If euthanasia is even to be considered – and to my surprise, no one who had recently coped with a dying parent wrote it off entirely – the decision must be left to individuals. The decision has to be personal. Because it's only at the personal level that love exists.

Corporations may have working partnerships; organizations may have historic links; governments may have policies. But only individuals are capable of love. I have considerable faith in the essential decency of persons towards those with whom they have a strong personal relationship.

If I'm going to trust my life to someone, I want it to be someone who is going to feel an enormous sense of loss when I die. If I'm going to trust my life to someone, I want that person to have enough emotional bonds to me that they will not discard me like a used Kleenex.

But it also has to be someone who cares deeply about *my* welfare. Someone who cares enough to let me go when the time is right, not someone who will keep me alive indefinitely to assuage his or her own feelings of guilt.

Living Wills

Along with revising our wills, Joan and I also drafted "Living Wills." To some extent, a Living Will is simply a request to be allowed to die with some dignity. In a deeper sense, it is an act of trust that goes beyond even a Power of Attorney. A Power of Attorney grants someone else authority over our possessions. The Living Will grants power over our lives. It says that when the time comes, we trust this person – we have chosen our daughter Sharon – to make the right decisions about keeping us going, or letting us go.

David Bryson

He wanted to go

Dad died in June 1997. By good fortune, it happened just as I arrived to visit with him in Scotland. Dad had a catheter problem and was rushed to hospital. His eyes were pained, as if he were asking, "Why the hell are we wasting time and money to fix me up? I just want to go." Thirty-six hours later, he contracted bronchial pneumonia. That's what takes a lot of people. He just passed out. He died two days later.

Surprisingly, we shed no tears. We knew he wanted to go, and we were all relieved for him.

Janice Leonard

Dad refused to take his pills

I don't know why dying has to be such a humiliating experience. But it is. Choice is taken away. When you're a self-sufficient person, it is terrible to have to suddenly rely on another person for everything. Your food. Your schedule. Even for wiping your bum. Dad would much rather die at home than in some kind of institution.

In the past, I could never understand why someone would want to call in Dr. Kevorkian, the doctor who helps people commit suicide, so that they can end their lives. But now I can begin to see it.

My dad wanted to end his life. He was rebelling against the discipline of the home. He refused to take his pills. So they now grind them up and put them in his applesauce, and he can't tell that he's taking them.

And After the Death

Your responsibilities don't end when your parent dies. In some ways, they're just beginning.

Although this is a book about caring for an elderly parent, you cannot escape the inevitable. Sooner or later, your parent will die. Death is the point at which all paths converge, before they open out again. There are innumerable ways for an aging person to lose his hair, her teeth, his mind, her strength… No two bodies are the same, and so no two people ever approach death in quite the same way.

For that reason, your experiences of caring for your aging parent will never be exactly the same as anyone else's. Whatever you do, however you do it, it's a one-time-only event. There are no rehearsals, and no reruns.

But death itself is universal. There is only one doorway, and everyone passes through it eventually.

For your parent, all the options, all the variables, have come to an end. But for you, the range of choices begins to open up immediately. Once again, you're faced with a bewildering multitude of choices. And once again, there are no precut templates you can apply. You have to play it by ear.

Even if you have no official responsibilities, this will be a busy period. You may not have time to do much grieving until after the funeral or memorial service.

Disposing of the body

Your first decision – assuming that you have been the primary caregiver and are now the executor – is to decide what to do with the body. If your religious community has specific traditions, that choice is already made for you. Muslims and Hindus, among others, have clearly defined customs for handling and disposing of the body.

Otherwise, you can choose cremation or burial. Cremation can be relatively inexpensive. The body doesn't need embalming, and can be cremated in a plain pine or even a cardboard coffin. Burial can be as expensive as you're willing to go – with embalming, walnut casket, prestigious plot…

I recommend cremation.

I don't worry that cremation will somehow deny the dead person a life after death. I believe that if God can grant new life to a body mashed up in an accident, or grant mobility to a body paralyzed since childhood, then a body reduced to ashes will pose no difficulties to God.

Each province or state has slightly varying legal requirements. Your doctor, your lawyer, a social worker, a government official – any of these can help you penetrate the thicket of regulations. Don't simply take the word of a funeral director. They're in business to make money for their firms, and may not always tell you the truth, the whole truth, and nothing but the truth. I've had funeral directors assure me – cross their heart and hope to die – that the law absolutely required embalming. It didn't.

Dealing with a funeral director

You probably will need a funeral director's services. Someone has to pick up your parent's body from the hospital, the nursing home, or your home. Someone has to do something with it. That's what funeral parlors are set up to do.

Any funeral parlor can give you a lavish funeral. They'll be delighted, because that's where they make their biggest profit. But if you don't want to spend more than necessary, I recommend dealing with a Memorial Society, if there's one around. Memorial Societies are organized to minimize both the hassles and the costs of funeral arrangements. They're generally efficient, and most of them won't try to sell you a more expensive service than you really want.

The paperwork will vary from province to province, from state to state. In British Columbia, we had to get a certificate from my father's doctor, formally stating the information about his death. We took that certificate, along with his birth certificate and some other identification, to the Memorial Society where Dad had been a member for more than 25 years. They handled all details of the cremation for us. They also arranged for an official death certificate.

The death certificate comes from a government registrar. You'll need it to close bank accounts, terminate insurance policies, claim benefits, change mailing addresses, and many other purposes. Our province uses the same form to register both deaths and marriages. Sharon looked at the form, looked at the registrar, and quipped, "Well, I guess you can count on at least 50 percent of these applications being permanent!"

Ultimately, you will need a dozen or more death certificates. If you get them through the official government registrar, you will pay a lot for them. It's cheaper and just as effective to get two official certificates, and then have a lawyer or notary public provide you with a handful of certified copies.

A funeral service

A funeral or memorial service is not mandatory. Some people never have one. And the urn of ashes sits disconsolately in a storage closet indefinitely. I think you should have some kind of service. We humans need rituals – even if they seem to be meaningless rituals at the time – to provide closure for an important period of our lives.

The kind of service you have will depend, again, on your faith tradition. If you're Muslim, Hindu, Jewish, Buddhist, or Christian, some of the rituals are prescribed for you. If you have no strong connections to any of these, you can pretty much arrange whatever you want.

If you want to have the body of your parent present, you need a funeral service. It can be in a church, or a funeral home. But the form of the service will be determined by the church's practices. If it's a Roman Catholic, Lutheran, or Anglican tradition, the service will probably include Mass or Eucharist, the service of Holy Communion. Almost any service will include some readings from that tradition's scriptures, along with a homily, sermon, or talk that deals – to a greater or lesser extent – with that tradition's beliefs about life, death, and continuing life. Depending on the setting, there may be songs or hymns. There may also be opportunity for personal tributes to the dead person, from friends or family members.

A funeral is commonly followed by a committal, where the body is placed in a grave. This can be a public event, a private event, or a non-event that no one goes to. It's up to you. You don't have to have a long procession of black cars with their lights on, threading their way through city streets to a cemetery. Unless you want one. You can be there, or you can leave the committal entirely to the persons organizing the funeral.

Don't let anyone rush you into a decision. A funeral or memorial service is not for the dead, but for the living. Your parent is gone. The service is for the survivors – for you, for your parent's relatives, and for ever-widening circles of friends and colleagues and associates.

A memorial service

If you don't want the body present, you can choose a memorial service instead of a funeral. A memorial service is almost always in a church, and follows more closely the pattern of a normal church service, with hymns and prayers. At the same time, a memorial service offers more freedom for a variety of personal tributes, and for a variety of songs and readings.

A funeral usually takes place within a few days of the death; a memorial service can be delayed for a week or more, to allow more time for people to gather.

Whether you have a formal funeral, a memorial service, or some other variation on a theme, the service leader will want to meet with you and other close family members, to find out what you want in the service. Some clergy will also do some unobtrusive grief counseling while meeting with you.

It helps if the person leading the service knew your parent. You may sit numbly through most of the service, still in shock, feeling the whole thing meaningless. But you may also find the leader speaking deep into your grief, and offering you a mental image you will clutch close to your heart for years after. Carolyn Pogue's book *Language of the Heart* (Northstone, 1998) describes how Marian Hood, an Alberta teacher and poet, was given the image of a plane, taking off into the sunrise, banking, its wings gleaming for a moment "with sunlight and burnished gold." Marian had not had a warm relationship with her father, but the minister's words gave her a new impression of him, which set her "on a search for my father." Alayne Scanlan received a different image. Her mother had had a wonderful laugh, the kind that lifted everyone's spirits who heard it. The minister taking the service, Bob Wallace, likened it to the ringing of a bell, "which in this life always has to stop, but which, in eternity, never needs to come to an end."

Although it's hard, when you're torn by conflicting emotions, try not to do anything in a funeral or memorial service that you will later wish you hadn't done. And don't talk yourself or let yourself get talked out of doing something that you would later wish you had done.

When Margaret Kyle's father died, her family had the memorial service just four days later. There were six children in the family. With the rush to get the service organized, there wasn't time to satisfy each person's hopes and wishes. Only one of the children, the oldest brother, spoke at the service; the rest kept quiet. "I kept thinking that people wouldn't be interested in hearing about his history, you know, some of the facts of his life, but I think now I was wrong," Margaret says. "When someone has lived for 80 years and more, there are a lot of good stories that could be told. Every one of us had special memories of Dad, but we kept quiet about them. We didn't even have pictures of him in the church.

"Afterwards, it's over so quickly, and you don't get a chance to go back and do anything differently."

Reception and recovery

You may also have a reception after the service. During the service, most of the people present have to be pretty passive. There's little opportunity for them to express their own feelings. The reception gives them a chance to have their say. Something about holding a cup of tea or coffee in one hand and a sticky-sweet brownie in the other encourages people to open up. It's like a smaller, short-term version of the Irish wake, where people tell stories about the one who died, and share their sense of loss.

If you've contracted with a funeral director, or any other organization, to run the service and the reception, they will probably provide a guest book. If you're doing it all yourself, you'll have to provide the guest book. Don't skip it. Signing their names and leaving messages of sympathy is part of the healing process of those attending the service.

Those who have never been through such a loss often expect you to be back to normal by the time the funeral or memorial service is over. Don't kid yourself. The process of grieving is just starting. And you will experience, all over again, most of the symptoms of grief that I described in Chapter 5. I said that I didn't cry much after my father's death. I wrote a letter to friend, wondering why I didn't feel utterly devastated by my father's death. It started out as a short letter, almost a note. Five single-spaced pages later, I realized I was mourning a lot more than I had thought I was.

Because I didn't cry much, I thought I wasn't grieving much. Then I caught myself pulling on extra sweaters, or wearing a coat indoors. I felt cold all the time. I felt tired all the time, too. A few times, I couldn't stop myself from going back to bed again after breakfast. And pulling the covers up over my head.

This was not my normal behavior. Rather, it reflected the turmoil of moving through a time of transition, from what had once been normal, to a "new normal" that didn't include my father in it.

The family gathers

Family members will have gathered for the funeral or memorial service. Aside from the service and reception, there may be other opportunities to get together.

You'll find that people react very differently to death. Those who have provided little care for your parent may demonstrate the greatest grief. By contrast, those who have spent the last months or years burning themselves out to provide care may feel mostly relief.

Just remember this: how much you weep for your parent is not a measure of how much you loved that person.

If all goes well, these family gatherings will be a time of reconciliation, of great warmth and mutual support. In the face of death, members of your family will set aside past differences. But they may not. This can also – regrettably – be a time for old feuds to surface. There may be recriminations. One child may have put the parent in a nursing home against the wishes of other children. There may be particularly strong feelings if one or two members of the family made the decision to pull the plug on an irreversible condition, and other members feel cheated of a last chance to connect with their parent.

Hostility and bitterness are the last thing you need at this time. You will find them devastating.

Even small setbacks can be shattering. And you will experience them. If not from your family, then from outsiders. Grief focuses you intensely inward, on your own inner suffering – suffering that the rest of the world is acutely unaware of. The day after my mother died, Dad and I went to pick up some groceries. I recall my sense of shock that shoppers in Safeway were going about their normal lives, as if nothing had happened. Similarly, a woman told me about her sense of outrage that the London trams were still running the morning after her father died!

After my father died, we had to clear out his room at Crofton Manor, to make it available for the next tenant. (A caretaker at Crofton told us many people don't bother clearing out a dead parent's room – they just abandon everything.) We loaded his chair, his desk, his dresser, his filing cabinet, his lamps, into our van and took them all back to his apartment. The building's regulations specified that all furniture moving must go through the basement door – which also meant carrying everything down a flight of stairs, around a sharp corner, and into a narrow hall to get it onto the elevator. But the front door was at ground level. We were in no condition, emotionally, to expend any unnecessary energy. So we parked on the street, loaded his possessions on a dolly, and wheeled them through the lobby to the elevator. One of the other residents of the building stopped us: "All moving must go through the basement door," he commanded.

We protested.

"Rules are rules," he snapped. And turning his back on our protests and our tears, he got onto our elevator ahead of us, closed the doors, and went up to his apartment.

It took us several hours to recover from that incivility.

The executor's tasks

If you're executor, you will have an apparently endless list of things to do.

First, notify everyone who needs to know about this death. Especially anyone or anything that provided income. Notify the bank. They'll freeze the accounts at once, but most banks will pay legitimate expenses associated with the disposal of the body and the funeral or memorial service. Notify any pension plans or annuities. Apply for any death benefits payable through pension plans or insurance policies. Cancel subscriptions, memberships, and credit cards. Register a change of address with the post office, to have your parent's mail forwarded to your address. Some places will simply take your word for the change. Others will require a copy of the death certificate. A few will want to see both the death certificate and the will. A very few – Canada Post is one – will require you to fill in their own multi-page forms, and attach notarized copies of other documents.

We listed every card or connection in Dad's wallet, desk, and bank box. We managed to reach most of them by phone within the first week. Generally speaking, they bent over backwards to cooperate. If they couldn't help directly, they helped us find the person or agency who could.

There are always exceptions, of course. We tried to reach the provincial medical plan by phone. I called eight to ten times a day, for three days. The line was always busy. I never even managed to get through to voice mail! So I sent a letter notifying them of Dad's death, and enclosed the premium invoice we had just received.

Two months later, we got a peremptory letter from the medical plan demanding immediate payment, or they would cut off Dad's medical services.

I did not take their demand kindly, I confess. "His ashes are sitting on the table in our front hall," my reply stormed. "Are they likely to require medical attention?"

I hope someone's face was red.

Second, you'll need to list your parent's assets and liabilities. Include everything. Car, TV, furniture, books, jewelry, art, stereo, stamp collection, even the golf ball autographed by Arnold Palmer... Yes, the chipped china in the kitchen cupboards too. And don't forget the house or condominium itself. Assign a value to every item. We bought a copy of the local "Buy and Sell" paper, and based the values on its classified ads. List the liabilities too: car loan, mortgage, credit card balances owing...

Now you're ready to apply to probate the will. Before you can start to act as executor, some court or level of government has to empower you.

You can apply for Letters Probate yourself. Many drugstores and stationery stores carry do-it-yourself kits containing the forms and instructions you need to guide you through the process. If it's a very simple will, you may want to go this route. Personally, I think it's worth hiring a lawyer (or, where they are permitted to perform the task, a notary), who is not emotionally involved in the process. Any legal pothole has the potential to reduce you to tears, especially if you're already a bit tattered around the heart.

The court will need to be sure that no one contests the will. It is unlikely to approve a will, for example, that bypasses a wife, giving her less than she's legally entitled to under provincial or state law. So copies of the will have to go to all who are, or might be, affected. If they want to contest the will, they have a defined period within which to take action. In British Columbia, it's six months.

If everything is in order, the court will issue Letters Probate – the title may vary from jurisdiction to jurisdiction, but this will serve for my purposes – and charge you a fee based on the value of your parent's estate. (Estates can usually pass without fee to a surviving spouse. But I have been assuming, in this book, that you had only one parent left. That's why you have been the primary caregiver.) Fees vary, from 0 to about 1.5 percent of the value of the estate. In British Columbia, the probate fee on a $200,000 estate would be about $2,600.

The Letters Probate affirm two things: a) that your parent's will is valid; b) that you're authorized to act as executor.

After the will is probated

Now you have access to your parent's bank box, accounts, investments, and property. You can put the house up for sale, and give the chipped china that no one wants to the Salvation Army.

But before you start handing out Lincoln limousines, there are still some legal hurdles. Your parent did not file a final income tax return. (Not even death permits escape from taxes!) As executor, you have to file a tax return on your parent's behalf, for the period from the beginning of the fiscal year up to the date of death. If your parent had minimal savings, and no income other than interest or government pension, you can probably do this return yourself. But very few parents have that simple a financial picture.

In Canada, some kinds of savings are tax sheltered. Registered retirement savings plans (RRSPs) can grow tax free. Registered retirement income funds (RRIFs) pay out those RRSPs over a period of years, with tax payable only on the amount actually withdrawn each year. But when your parent dies, any RRSPs or RRIFs remaining are treated as if they had been totally cashed in, all at once. Every cent is taxable. That can amount to a huge hunk of liability.

In Canada, a house or principal residence is usually tax exempt. But next to nothing else is. Your parent's final tax return has to calculate how much stamp or coin collections, antique furniture or cars, and shares in corporations or mutual funds, may have gained or lost in value. And that's on top of the usual complications of income tax forms: tax credits, deductions, charitable donations, medical benefits... If you find ordinary income tax forms difficult, don't try to do the final return yourself. Unless it's a very simple estate, I recommend hiring a professional – if not to do the actual return, at least to provide advice. It will cost money; it's worth the expense.

Pay the bills

After the final income tax return has been completed and accepted, you can apply for a statement from the tax authorities that the estate no longer owes anything to the government. Not until you've received such a statement – in Canada, it's called a Clearance Certificate – should you start writing checks to beneficiaries. Otherwise, you could divide up the estate, and then find that you didn't have enough left to pay the final income tax bill. It's very hard to get money back after you've handed it out. You could end up having to absorb the entire tax bill yourself, with nothing left to compensate you for your years of care.

Additionally, when money is paid out to a beneficiary, you should obtain a Release from the beneficiary prior to payment. The Release says, in effect, that beneficiary will make no further claims against the estate.

Finally, you should consider placing advertisements in a local paper to protect yourself from potential creditors.

As I write these paragraphs, I have not yet tidied up the final details of my father's estate. I'm not sure when everything will be completed. Some estates can take years to settle, especially if one or more of the beneficiaries decides to contest the will. I estimate that, before it's all over, I will have paid out up to $10,000 in legal and accounting fees. I consider it worth every penny.

When all the work is done

And when it's all done... In fact, I suspect it's *never* "all done." Jack McCarthy, publisher of our local community newspaper, told me, "My dad died ten years ago, and there's not a day goes by that I don't think of him. Even yet – not a day."

I find I still miss my mother – though not every day – and she died 28 years ago. I have no doubt that I shall feel the loss of my father for many years, perhaps for the rest of my life.

Such feelings are almost inevitable. These are, after all, the people who gave you life. They knew you before anyone else did.

After my father's death, I realized that a lot of the pain I was feeling had to do with a loss of my own roots. There was no one left to tell me where I came from.

I remembered my sense of shock when I first learned that Dad had proposed to another woman, before my mother. She hadn't wanted to be a missionary, so she turned him down. I realized that if she had said yes, I wouldn't be here. They might have had a child, but it wouldn't have been me.

Now that I have no parents left, I can't ask about what I did, what I learned, how I reacted, in those early years before my own memory started functioning. I can't find out if there were any words that I constantly mispronounced, who I played with, what my favorite toys were, how I adapted to living in various locations... I can't ask about childhood illnesses, visitors to our home, my parents' relationship with each other, the effects of the War...

After my mother died, I remember writing to her sister, my aunt, lamenting that I didn't really know my mother. It sounds silly to say that, but I didn't. So much lay hidden in the past, in stories and experiences I never heard. My aunt wrote back with some basic facts, but it wasn't facts I wanted – it was personality. Her childhood. Why she chose to teach English. Why she decided to go to India. What thrilled her, and what disappointed her.

But I wasn't really asking about my mother. I was asking about me.

The death of the last parent has forced me to an uncomfortable conclusion. I can no longer look to anyone else for answers or explanations. I have to accept myself as I am, with a lot of myself unknown. I can't look for causes or patterns in what I don't know about. I am what I am, and that's that.

The rest is a closed book.

Like this one.

Gloria Cope

Mourning in community

My aboriginal friend, Jill Harris, invited me to her home on the Penelakut Reserve for a traditional ceremony in honor of her family's ancestors. Jill's father had passed away a year earlier, so his memory especially would be honored this evening.

Family members and close friends gathered together on the grounds behind Jill's house.

I watched with fascination when her brothers began to prepare the table that would be used for the great feast. Finished, it would measure four feet by twenty, large enough to allow for at least 20 place settings. Firewood was stacked underneath the table, plugging every available crevice, with bits of newspaper stuffed here and there. Several women were busy preparing the food. Turkey, vegetables, mashed potatoes and other hot dishes were cooked inside, while other delights such as pie, oranges, rolls, and cold drinks had already been placed outdoors.

In anticipation, we stood huddled together for protection against November's cool crisp wind.

Before long, all was ready and the ceremony began. The women began to serve the meal. I learned that custom dictates that the eldest living family member speaks the traditional blessing. Singing in her native tongue, Jill's auntie portrayed a priestly role with superb humility and grace, extending her arms upward to the heavens, offering symbolic food to their ancestors. A plate in each hand, she repeated the ritual until all who had been called to the great spirit table were served.

Family members who could remember a favorite food of their ancestor shared this with the women who dished out the various helpings. It was fun to watch as they added an extra orange or two or a huge helping of mashed potatoes and gravy. I laughed when I saw three rolls on one plate. Extra helpings of everything were then placed down the center of the table.

I watched in wonder as Jill's brother took the torch he was carrying and set aflame the wood that had been placed underneath the freshly laden table. The soulful sounds of a people in mourning began to take over the rhythm of the chant.

Unexpectedly, out of the darkness, came the image of my own mother's face. She had died without warning two months earlier in southern Ontario. Mom's "celebration of life" service had taken place four days later, and within a week I was back home on Vancouver Island feeling empty and sad. It seemed to me at the time there should be something more to do in living out the grief process. Could this be a time for me to do so? Holding her image close, I shut my eyes tight and embraced her sweet and loving memory.

At this moment, Jill, standing next to me, whispered, "Gloria, bring your mother to the table. There is plenty of food for guests." On hearing this, my eyes overflowed with tears as I wept from the depth of my being.

Later, as the last embers of fire burned away, this community of people, spent and hungry, went into the house where fellowship continued over yet another table laden with food.

Carolynn Honor
The right thing to say

I was celebrating my 50th birthday, when the home called to say that my mother was slipping. We got the message and headed right up there. It was 11:00 p.m. when we arrived. I spent the night there; my husband Peter came home to the kids. Peter had to get up to go to work in the morning; I didn't. The next day I did an evening shift, nursing, and then went back to the nursing home again for another night.

She seemed to be okay. So I went home for a rest.

Almost immediately, we got another call to say that she was slipping fast, and we should come right now. Peter and I both went up. We went into the room. I said, "Hi Mum," and started talking, the way I usually did. For the last while, she didn't know who I was. She thought I was her sister. "If that's the way you want it," I had decided, "then that's who I'll be for today." I was getting pretty good at this after three years.

And she took a breath, and didn't take another.

The nurse on duty said, "It's just as if she had been waiting for you."

Bless her, it was exactly the right thing to say. I don't know if she said it to everyone, or just to me, but it was exactly the right thing to say to me at that time.

❧

APPENDIX ONE

Hiring In-Home Help

A guide developed by the Family Caregiver Alliance of San Francisco.

Most caregivers of persons with cognitive disorders reach a point when they need help at home. Telltale signs include recognizing that the impaired person requires constant supervision and/or assistance with everyday activities of daily living. Caregivers also find that certain housekeeping routines and regular errands are accomplished with great difficulty or are left undone. It may become apparent that in order to take care of any business outside the home, a substitute care provider is needed.

Exploring home-care options

A number of options are available to caregivers for finding help at home. It is possible to hire a helper from a home health agency (listed in the yellow pages of local telephone directories). Many caregivers, however, find it is more affordable to hire an in-home helper privately. With some foresight and careful planning, it is possible for the caregiver to locate the right person for the job.

For caregivers in California, the local Caregiver Resource Center is available to assist in determining what kind of help would be most useful and what types of resources are available in each community.

Writing a job description

An important first step in hiring in-home help is to determine what help is needed and to prepare a list of duties the caregiver would like carried out. This job description should be designed as a work contract which can be signed by both the caregiver and the in-home helper.

Typical duties for an in-home helper include companionship and supervision of the impaired person and direct assistance with personal care such as bathing, dressing and feeding. The in-home helper may also do light housekeeping and home maintenance tasks which pertain directly to the care of the impaired person or which the caregiver can no longer manage without assistance.

A good work contract should include the following:
- Name of employer and "household employee"
- Wages and benefits (e.g., mileage, meals, etc.)
- When and how payment will be made
- Hours of work
- Employee's Social Security number
- Duties to be performed
- Unacceptable behavior (e.g., smoking, abusive language, etc.)
- Termination (how much notice, reasons for termination without notice, etc.)
- Dated signatures of employee and employer

Looking for help at home

The next step is to find the appropriate person to fit the job description. One of the best ways of finding a helper is to get a personal recommendation from a trusted relative or friend. Churches, synagogues, senior centers, Independent Living Centers and local college career centers, especially those which have nursing or social work programs, are good places to advertise for in-home help.

Most communities have attendant registries which are an excellent resource for finding in-home help because they typically provide some initial screening of applicants. When calling an attendant registry, it is important to inquire about their particular screening process and/or training requirements as well as about any fees charged. While some are free, fees for using a registry can vary greatly. There are also nonprofit community agencies that maintain lists of individuals available to perform all kinds of household tasks, from cleaning and laundry to repairs and gardening. It is a good idea to shop around and obtain the best service for the lowest fee.

If all of the above sources fail to produce an in-home helper, the caregiver may choose to advertise in the "Help Wanted" classified section of a community college or local newspaper or newsletter. The advertisement, at the minimum, should include hours, a brief description of duties, telephone number and best time to call.

Interviewing the applicant

The caregiver does not have to personally interview every person who applies for the job. Some screening over the telephone is appropriate. In screening applicants over the telephone, caregivers should describe the job in detail and state specific expectations listed in the work contract as well as information about the hours and wages. At this time it is also important to ask about the applicant's past experience and whether he/she has references. Then if the applicant sounds acceptable, an interview should be scheduled.

In preparation for the interview, the caregiver should have a list of questions pertinent to the job description and a sample work contract ready for the applicant to read. The following are some suggested questions for the interview:

- Where have you worked before?
- What were your duties?
- How do you feel about caring for an elderly/disabled person? Or a person with memory problems?
- Have you had experience cooking for other people?
- How do you handle people who are angry, stubborn, fearful?
- Do you have a car? Would you be able to transfer someone from a wheelchair into a car or onto a bed?
- Is there anything in the job description that you are uncomfortable doing?
- What time commitment are you willing to make to stay on the job?
- Can you give me two work-related and one personal reference?

Immediately after the interview, it is important for the caregiver to write down first impressions, and if possible, discuss these with another family member or friend. Consider the person most qualified for the job and with whom you feel most comfortable. *Always* check the references of at least two final applicants. Don't wait too long to make the offer, as good applicants may find another job. If the offer is accepted, the caregiver and the in-home helper should set a date to sign the contract and begin work. Both employer and employee should keep a copy of the contract.

Investigating legal issues

As an employer of a "household employee," there are several legal considerations. First, household employers should verify that their household insurance (renter's or homeowner's) covers household employees in case of an accident. It is also imperative that the employer be fully informed of the legal responsibility of paying taxes for household employees.

[Editor's note: Provinces and states will all have their own laws about employing a person within a household. Generally speaking, unless the services are provided by a government agency, or unless you contract with some other organization which actually employs the home care worker, you become the employer, and must obey all applicable laws. These may include withholding a portion of payments to cover taxes, payment of mandatory benefits, etc. Check with your local labor offices before signing anything with anyone.]

Printed with permission of Family Caregiver Alliance, San Francisco. For more information, see website **http://www.caregiver.org.**

APPENDIX TWO

Checklist for Administering an Estate

Based on information provided by Alfred H. Field of MacQuarrie Hobkirk Barristers and Solicitors, Vancouver, British Columbia, in turn based on publications of the People's Law School, Vancouver, British Columbia.

The administration of an estate involves a number of tasks. Whether or not you personally attend to each of these, or you hire a lawyer to act on your behalf, the following list will give you a general idea of what an executor is required to do.

Locate the will

- Look through important papers kept by the deceased at home or at a place of business.
- Check the safety deposit box at the bank or at any trust companies the deceased may have dealt with.
- Apply to the Wills Registry for a Wills Search in all possible names the deceased may have used.
- Apply for a Death Certificate.

Arrange for the funeral and for disposition of the deceased's body

Arrange for the immediate financial requirements of dependent survivors

- Notify insurance companies of death; complete and submit claim forms.
- Arrange for transfer of joint bank accounts.
- Contact employer, and obtain any wages owing at the date of death.

Notify appropriate agencies of the death

- Notify pension offices, banks, employer, life insurance companies.
- Cancel any subscriptions or memberships of the deceased.
- Cancel charge accounts.

Find and determine all assets of the deceased

- Write to banks, trust companies, credit unions, stock brokerage firms and other financial institutions the deceased may have dealt with for information on accounts.
- Take an inventory of the deceased's safety deposit box.
- Check for any insurance policies or RRSPs.
- Contact pension offices for estimate of pension benefits and apply for Canada Pension Plan death benefit, survivor's or orphan's benefits, if eligible.
- Search through all personal papers of the deceased to find any real estate or business interests and obtain current valuations.
- List and value all household goods and furnishings.
- List and value all personal effects, including cars, boats, jewelry, etc.
- Check with the deceased's employer for any money owing to the deceased, including any death benefits, if applicable.
- Check for any other debts owing to the deceased.

Find and determine all liabilities of the deceased

- List funeral and burial expenses and any outstanding medical expenses.
- Check all ongoing accounts such as charge accounts and utility bills.
- Review real estate holdings for any mortgages.
- Check with banks, trust companies, and any other financial institutions the deceased may have dealt with for any outstanding loans.

- Estimate the income tax payable up to the date of death.
- Advertise for creditors by publishing a notice in a local newspaper.

Prepare a complete inventory of all assets and liabilities of the deceased

Safeguard the assets

- Review insurance policies and provide adequate coverage for all property.
- Take valuables into custody or obtain secured storage.

Apply for grant of Letters Probate

- Notify all potential beneficiaries of intent to apply for probate and entitlement under the will.
- Notify persons who would be heirs-at-law under an intestacy, and persons eligible to apply under the *Wills Variation Act*.
- Submit properly completed and executed documents, statements, and affidavits, and appropriate filing and probate fees.

Apply for benefits, and transfer property into your name

- Apply to Canada Post for redirection of the deceased's mail to the executor.
- Submit all claims for proceeds of life insurance or other insurance policies.
- Apply for eligible Canada Pension Plan death, survivor's, or orphan's benefits.
- Apply for proceeds from RRSPs or other private pension plans.
- Apply for Civil Service, Union, or Veteran's benefits, if applicable.
- Transfer ownership of all registered property, such as real estate, into your name.
- Add your name to the house and car insurance and all other property insurance.

Prepare and file tax returns

- Locate the last income tax return of the deceased.
- File the deceased's income tax returns for the year of death, and any previous years as necessary.
- File an income tax return for the estate, for the period following the death of the deceased.

Pay all debts and expenses

- Pay funeral expenses and all taxes payable, such as income tax or municipal taxes on property.
- Pay all legal and accounting fees and other expenses in administering the estate.
- Reimburse yourself for reasonable out-of-pocket expenses and pay your fee as executor, if applicable.
- Pay any other outstanding debts of the deceased.
- Sell assets to obtain sufficient cash for payments.

Distribute the estate

- Wait six months from the Grant of Letters Probate for any applications under the *Wills Variation Act.*
- Keep proper accounting records of everything you have done and pass your accounts for approval by the beneficiaries.
- Obtain Clearance Certificates from Revenue Canada that all income taxes have been paid.
- Sell assets at your discretion.
- Pay out all cash legacies and deliver items of property that have been specifically bequested.
- Distribute the residue or balance of the estate to beneficiaries.
- Obtain releases from the beneficiaries.

Agencies and Organizations Related to Aging, Health Care, and Incontinence

A Canadian Aging and Caregiving Resource Guide

The Caregiver Network has published on the Internet an exhaustive listing of Canadian agencies, organizations, and services available to those providing care for an aging person. The listing includes the names and phone numbers of both federal and provincial organizations and agencies, as well as organizations representing the needs of those with specific health concerns, such as diabetes, Alzheimers, or Parkinson's disease.

The Caregiver Network has included in this list an exhaustive bibliography, as well a directory of website addresses.

The Canadian *Aging and Caregiving Resource Guide* can be found at **http://www.caregiver.on.ca.**

In the USA

The United States, being about ten times more populous than Canada, has about ten times more agencies and organizations dealing with caregiving for elders. Kimberly-Clark has published a useful listing of selected American associations and organizations on its Depends website.

The listing begins with a directory of incontinence associations, including Bladder Health Council and the June Allyson Foundation. Keep scrolling and you'll find contact information for many other health-issue-related agencies – including the Alzheimer's Association, the American Diabetes Association, and the American Parkinson's Disease Association.

This list of resources can be found at **http://www.depend.com/ incont_edu_center/support groups/organizations.** You can also access the listing by going to the **http://www.kimberly-clark.com** site map and clicking on the "Adult Care" and "Incontinence Education Center" links.

Two other websites are worth mentioning. ThirdAge.com is intended for "older adults." The site covers a wide range of interests and topics, including care of aging parents. Information is available through interactive formats, such as chat rooms, as well as through articles and other features. The address is **http://www.ThirdAge.com.**

ElderWeb, the second site, includes nearly 4,500 reviewed links to long-term care information. It was designed to be a research site for both professionals and family members looking for information on eldercare. The address is **http://www.elderweb.com.**

BIBLIOGRAPHY

Current Books

Avery, Wilma J. *Sickness, Death, and Tears: Home Care for the Terminally Ill.*
PineCrest Press, 1994. (1937 – 156 Street, Surrey, BC, Canada V4A 4T7)
Published as a mourning project for the author's husband. Not a very
sophisticated-looking publication, but with lots of good ideas and
suggestions, especially for those providing home care for cancer patients.

Choosing an Executor – Being an Executor. People's Law School, 1996.
(Suite 150, 900 Howe Street, Vancouver, BC, Canada V6Z 2M4)
A simple, clear guide to the tasks and responsibilities of an executor.
The basis for the checklist shown in Appendix 3.

Foster, Sandra E. *You Can't Take It with You: The Common-Sense Guide to
Estate Planning for Canadians.* Second ed. Toronto: John Wiley and Sons
Canada, 1998.
Although intended primarily for seniors themselves, this guide
contains a wealth of information about wills, probate fees, powers of
attorney, and responsibilities of an executor. Very specific to Canada,
with an abundance of illustrations reflecting various provincial laws and
contexts.

Gager, Dorothy. *Parenting Your Parents.* A LifeSearch book, Nashville: Abingdon Press, 1996.

LifeSearch books focus on group study, with information for input, points for discussion, and related Bible study topics. Helpful for those seeking a Christian faith perspective in their experiences with aging parents.

Grollman, Earl, and Sharon Grollman. *Your Aging Parents: Reflections for Caregivers.* Boston: Beacon Press, 1997.

Earl Grollman is the guru of grieving. This book, republished from 1978, contains short meditations and reflections on changing relationships between parent and child, based on experience. Insightful, often moving. But don't expect much practical advice on legal or financial matters.

Jones-Lee, A., and Melanie Callendar. *The Complete Guide to Eldercare.* New York: Barrons, 1998.

Barrons is an educational publisher, so this book concentrates on useful information. The writing tends to be plodding but thorough. Especially valuable for its section on nursing homes and other institutional care.

Lebow, Grace, and Barbara Kane, with Irwin Lebow. *Coping with Your Difficult Older Parent: A Guide for Stressed-Out Children.* New York: Avon Books, 1999.

Difficult reading, because it's filled with depressing case studies of difficult and even malicious parents. But if that's what you have to cope with, this book could be a lifesaver. Lots of psychological analysis, suggestions for action.

Lustbader, Wendy, and Nancy R. Hooyman. *Taking Care of Aging Family Members: A Practical Guide.* New York: The Free Press, division of Simon and Schuster, 1994.

A comprehensive and thorough book. Each chapter includes an extensive list of supplementary resources. One of the most useful elements may be the various charts and tables you can use as checklists.

Manning, Doug. *Parenting Our Parents.* In-Sight Books, 1989.
(P.O. Box 42467, Oklahoma City, OK 73125)
Short booklet, part of a Continuing Care Series. Helpful as a handout.
Good anecdotal illustrations of the problems of role reversals. Manning
also has a video series, and several other books on aging, all available
through In-Sight's website, **http://www.insightbooks.com**

Mitford, Jessica. *The American Way of Death Revisited.* New York: Alfred A.
Knopf, 1998.
Mitford's book about American funeral practices, customs, and
taboos first burst upon an unsuspecting public in 1963. Revised and
updated, it's still a worthwhile read.

Molloy, William. *What Are We Going to Do Now? Helping Your Parents in
Their Senior Years.* Toronto: Key Porter Books, 1998.
Considers senior care primarily from a medical viewpoint. Valuable
information, especially about medication and depression. Molloy is the
only author who defines Advance Medical Directives, which are more
comprehensive than the usual Living Will. The writing can be plodding;
it comes alive when Molloy writes about his own experience with his
dying parents.

Morris, Virginia. *How to Care for Aging Parents.* New York: Workman
Publishing, 1996. Published in Canada by Thomas Allen & Son Limited.
An exhaustive and well-written text, loaded with insights and information. Designed with lots of sidebars and checklists. Almost every page
will provide a useful insight. The chapters are applicable to almost any
situation; the reference material at the back is massive and comprehensive, although the organizations and addresses are exclusively United
States based. Morris is a journalist, and writes with a journalist's skill, so
the book is never dull.

Moskowitz, Francine & Robert. *Parenting Your Aging Parents.* Los Angeles: Key Publications, 1991.

The book has recently been turned into an e-mail study program that provides 30- to 60-year-olds – the so-called "Sandwich Generation" – with information to help their aging parents maintain a satisfactory quality of life in the face of illness, disability, and decline. Book and course cover Issues of Responsibility, Housing, Finances, Medical Care, Emotional Issues, Family Issues, and Death-Related Issues. The diseases and disabilities are universal, the rest comes mainly with a U.S. perspective. E-mail: Robertam@ix.netcom.com

Pogue, Carolyn. *Language of the Heart: Rituals, Stories, and Information about Death.* Kelowna, BC, Canada: Northstone Publishing, 1998.

This book provides help for those planning a unique funeral or memorial service for a loved one. It answers the most commonly asked questions, and provides lots of creative suggestions and sample service outlines.

Taylor, James. *Letters to Stephen.* Kelowna, BC, Canada: Northstone Publishing, 1996. (Previously published as *Surviving Death,* Winfield, BC: Wood Lake Books Inc., 1993.)

An exploration of grief. Prompted by, but not by any means limited to, the death of the author's son, of cystic fibrosis. Has been used by counselors to assist with grief resulting from corporate downsizing, loss of parents, loss of employment, etc. Makes the subject personal and compelling.

Some favorites from the past are
worth remembering and rereading, too

Kübler-Ross, Elisabeth. *On Death and Dying*. New York: MacMillan Publishing, 1969 and reprints.

> The pioneering book that looked at how terminally ill patients get ready to die. If it's not available, many of Kübler-Ross's subsequent books pick up the same themes.

Kushner, Harold. *When Bad Things Happen to Good People*. New York: Avon Books, 1981 and reprints.

> Kushner's focus was shaped by the death of his son, but the themes he develops apply to any situation where an innocent victim seems to be suffering.

Lewis, C. S. *A Grief Observed*. Minneapolis, MN: Seabury Press, Winchester Press, 1961.

> An extremely intimate chronicle of Lewis' grief upon the death of his wife from cancer.

Nouwen, Henri. *The Wounded Healer*. New York: Image/Doubleday, 1979.

> How the suffering you experience as a caregiver can prove healing for both yourself and others. A theological approach to suffering.

Wangerin, Walter, Jr. *Mourning into Dancing*. Grand Rapids, MI: Zondervan, 1992.

> Storytelling is Wangerin's forte. Here he builds his stories around the death of his father.

ACKNOWLEDGMENT OF PERMISSIONS GRANTED

September Song, by Maxwell Anderson and Kurt Weill.
TRO – © Copyright 1938 (renewed), Hampshire House Publishing Corp. and Chappell & Co. for the USA. All rights for the World excluding the USA controlled by Chappell & Co. All Rights Reserved. Used by permission.

In-Sight Books, P.O. Box 42467, Oklahoma City, OK 73125, for permission to quote from *Parenting Our Parents* by Doug Manning.

Alfred Field, MacQuarrie and Hobkirk Barristers and Solicitors, #2020 – 777 Hornby Street, Vancouver, BC V6Z 1T9, and Gordon Hardy, The People's Law School, #150 – 900 Howe Street, Vancouver, BC V6Z 2M4, for permission to adapt their materials into Appendix 3, A Checklist for Administering an Estate.

Bonnie Lawrence, Family Caregiver Alliance, 425 Bush Street, Suite 500, San Francisco, CA 94108, for permission to reprint portions of their guidelines for hiring in-home help as Appendix 1.

Elizabeth Barker, David Bryson, Jeannette Buchholz, John Congram, Gloria Cope, Diane Forrest, Carolynn Honor, David Keating, Janice Leonard, Doug Moore, Terry Samuel, John Shearman, Wendy Smallman, and Elaine Towgood, for permission to include parts of their stories. It was not possible to trace some Internet contributors who used either nicknames or no identification at all.

INDEX